To **Hélène Connor,** whose dedication to
a better world inspired this book.

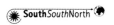

DOUBLE
STOREY
a juta company

SouthSouthNorth

iTDG
PUBLISHING

CLIMATE

AND THE KYOTO PROTOCOL'S **CLEAN DEVELOPMENT MECHANISM**

CHANGE

BRAZIL | BANGLADESH | INDONESIA | SOUTH AFRICA

Margie Orford

With Stefan Raubenheimer and Barry Kantor

ACKNOWLEDGMENTS

Many deserve thanks for helping SouthSouthNorth get this far and for enabling a book which captures a glimpse of our journey. Our sincere gratitude goes to the SouthSouthNorth country teams, all who have worked with and supported us, our project participants for sticking by us, and our country governments for giving us the opportunity to contribute.

This book was made possible through funding of the SouthSouthNorth Trust by the Ministry of Foreign Affairs Development Assistance of the Government of the Netherlands.

Grateful thanks go to the Trustees of the SouthSouthNorth Trust:

Michael Radomsky
Somasundran Naidoo
Ogunlade Davidson
Bambang Susantono
Eduardo Sales Novaes
Syed Iqbal Ali

For details on all the projects go to:
www.southsouthnorth.org

The implementing agencies of SouthSouthNorth are:

Brazil: Alberto Luiz Coimbra Institute of Post Graduate Studies and Research in Engineering, Federal University of Rio de Janeiro, www.coppe.ufrj.br
Bangladesh: The Bangladesh Centre for Advanced Studies, Dhaka, www.bcas.net
Indonesia: Pelangi, Jakarta, www.pelangi.or.id
South Africa: Krysalis, Cape Town, www.southsouthnorth.org

Published 2004 by ITDG Publishing,
103 -105 Southampton Row,
London WC1B 4HL, UK,
and in 2003 by Double Storey Books,
a division of Juta & Co. Ltd,
Mercury Crescent, Wetton, Cape Town,
in association with SouthSouthNorth,
138 Waterkant Street, Cape Town,
South Africa.

© 2003 SouthSouthNorth

ISBN 1 919930 51 5 (Double Storey)
ISBN 1 85339 593 5 (ITDG Publishing)

All rights reserved.

A catalogue record for this book is
available from the British Library.

Photographs: Margie Orford

Children's art workshop developed by
Jane Solomon, Cape Town.

Designed by CHALK DESIGN
5a Carstens Street, Tamboerskloof,
Cape Town, South Africa

Printed in South Africa by Mills Litho,
Cape Town.

CONTENTS

FOREWORD

The idea for this story emerged late one night. While deeply involved in the analytic interpretation of the Kyoto Protocol texts, applying the highly technical requirements of the Clean Development Mechanism to our project activities, the question arose: What about the people we meet, whose lives we touch? This is the story of a journey – about the hearts and hopes of those who are involved with SouthSouthNorth. It will speak to anyone who is interested in the problems of development and in the future of our planet. It will interest developers and investors, energy users and energy producers, governments of the developed and of the developing world.

Global warming is a dire threat to life. Yet it has so far entered just a small way into the collective consciousness. It is a tortoise to the current world's hares of digital wars and viral outbreaks. It is a giant risk often ignored because of its insidious progression, the enormity of our fears, and the power of vested interests. The global community has yet to take into account the real costs of consumerism and to properly govern our relationship with nature. We are now at the brink of a new era, where social and environmental accounting must become a central part of all economic endeavours. In this new world, sustainable development is the key tool for our very survival.

The ongoing difficulties in negotiating the content of the Kyoto Protocol and bringing it to ratification bear witness to the enormity of the task of stabilising our climate, and the great number of players who need to co-operate to achieve this aim. The Clean Development Mechanism gives rich and poor countries an opportunity to combine forces through projects in the developing world: this complex trade mechanism is unique in its promotion of sustainable development. SouthSouthNorth is an experiment in four countries to achieve this.

We are interdependent – when you switch on a light in Africa, you affect a person in Europe, a tree in South America, a coral reef in Australia, an island community in the Pacific. To be successful in dealing with global warming, we must be accountable – taking account of poverty, of technology, of society and of our environment. Only then will we be accounting for the generations to come.

Stefan Raubenheimer
C.E.O. SouthSouthNorth

Barry Kantor
Communications and Media SouthSouthNorth

HOW THIS BOOK WAS MADE

These stories of the developing world were related to me in a series of conversations in offices, over dinner, in rickshaws and on rubbish dumps. I am not a scientist so my questions were not technical ones. They were shaped by my desire to know why people were doing this difficult, time-consuming work; about how they coaxed investors into trying new ideas; about when to draw communities into trying new technologies to mitigate the arcane threat of climate change.

At the heart of these stories is passion and, folded into the centre of each of them, is a vision of the future. This book accounts for the poetry and passion that inspires the people in the SouthSouthNorth network to transform the dry language of an international climate change treaty into measurable improvements in people's lives in the South that simultaneously offer the global gift of reducing the emission of greenhouse gases. It is intangibles – humour, trust, friendship – that inform and give heart to the knowledge gleaned from considered projects meticulously designed. This work shows how the elegant creativity of science can be stitched with the delightful unpredictability of politics and human behaviour. The projects and approach of each country coalesced quite naturally into technology, poverty alleviation, social justice and the protection of the environment, that together are the pillars of sustainable development. Thus Brazil, with its highly technical projects, is the chapter which 'accounts' for technology. Bangladesh with its energetic but abjectly poor people is the chapter that 'accounts' for poverty. Indonesia, balancing the pressure of people on a fragile habitat, 'accounts' for the environment. South Africa 'accounts' for people, for social justice, as the country transforms itself beyond the divisions of apartheid.

A book on climate change needs to hold in the present the questions 'why', 'how' and 'what can be done' (questions I hope the reader will keep with them) to do justice to the experimental texture of SouthSouthNorth's experience. This resulted in an open-ended collage of personal stories and images structured around the spine of the hands on process of implementing projects. These bring direct benefits now, but their intention is to reduce greenhouse gas emissions to assure our collective future.

But what does that future look like? To whom does it belong? I asked children to do mandalas of themselves in the world and the world in them. I also asked groups of children to map their own environments. In both I asked the children to show both the present and the future. These artworks were an unexpectedly generous gift. Generated in workshops held in Bengali, Javanese, Indonesian, Xhosa, Portuguese and English, they provide a rare insight into children's understanding of their places in the world now, and how they imagine their futures will be. These pictures, some humorous, others grave, many joyful and quirky, a few exquisite jewels of colour and insight – resonate with SouthSouthNorth's endeavour to assure for these children the futures they assume to be theirs.

Margie Orford

3

CLIMATE CHANGE: the problem

From the industrial revolution onwards human activity has drawn increasingly vast amounts of energy from fossil fuels out of the earth. Burning these fossil fuels releases exponentially growing emissions of greenhouse gases into our atmosphere.

Science shows that these gases are accumulating, warming the earth beyond expectation and changing the delicate balance of the world's climate.

All of nature and people all over the world will suffer the impacts of climate change. These are already being felt. Droughts, increasing desertification, floods, coral-bleaching and storms will become more frequent and more severe. People urgently need to take responsibility for reducing greenhouse gas emissions for the well being of future generations.

Greenhouse gases trap infrared radiation emitted by the earth's surface, thus warming the earth and the atmosphere that protects it. These gases include carbon dioxide (CO_2), methane (CH_4), nitrous oxide (N_2O), hydrofluorocarbons (HFC), perfluorocarbons (PFC) and sulphur hexafluoride (SF_6).

Since 1750, the atmospheric concentrations of carbon dioxide have increased by 30%, methane by 145%, and nitrous oxide by 15%. This could lead to a mean global temperature rise of 13.5° centigrade by the end of this century, higher than that experienced over the last ten thousand years. Such a rise may lead to changes in the global atmospheric system, shifts in the climatic zones, increasingly extreme and changed mean weather conditions. It could also lead to the melting of glaciers and a rise in the sea level of between fifteen centimetres and one metre. These shifts are referred to as the climate change phenomenon.

CLIMATE CHANGE: the world responds

Reducing emissions is a gigantic and expensive task. It requires a comprehensive overhaul of the energy economy, with dramatic changes in our provision and consumption of energy. Other sources of greenhouse gas, such as methane from our vast waste dumps, must also be prevented from polluting the atmosphere.

When world leaders faced these issues at the United Nations Conference on Environment and Development of 1992 in Rio de Janeiro, they started one of the most difficult negotiations in history. In a first response, United Nations members signed the Framework Convention on Climate Change, in which member countries committed themselves to the problem through voluntary efforts to reduce greenhouse gas emissions and to increase the extent of natural systems such as forests that could absorb them.

After 1992 our understanding of the science of global warming moved to greater levels of certainty. Voluntary action proved inadequate as predictions revealed ever more frightening consequences. Hence binding obligations had to be imposed. A set of targets was proposed by the United Nations member states in the 1997 Kyoto Protocol. Although small, the targets set were seen as a positive beginning. Subsequently negotiations about full agreement on these binding targets and on procedures for achieving them have continued.

Not all countries have agreed to ratify the Kyoto Protocol. More than a decade after the United Nations Conference on Environment and Development, we are still struggling to achieve consensus and find solutions that respond to the serious challenges faced by multi-lateralism.

At the third Conference of the Parties of the United Nations Framework Convention on Climate Change, the Kyoto Protocol was adopted. The Protocol aims to reduce the emissions of developed countries (known as Annex 1 or the 'North') by at least 5% below their respective 1990 levels, and in some cases 1995 levels, in the period 2008 - 2012.

Individually, these countries have separate commitments. The European Union countries are collectively expected to reduce their emissions by 8%, the United States of America by 7% and Japan by 6%. Australia, Iceland and Norway are allowed to increase their emissions. The remaining countries are allowed varying levels of reduction. Although an important first step, it falls short of what is needed to stabilise global concentrations of greenhouse gases.

5

THE CLEAN DEVELOPMENT MECHANISM

In the Climate Change Convention, the Industrialised countries of the North agreed that they bore the responsibility to be the first group of countries to bind themselves to emission reduction targets because their historically accumulated emissions were greater than those of the developing countries of the South. During the negotiations, this group of countries grappled with ways to reduce the tremendously high anticipated cost of reaching these targets and agreed to various forms of mutual co-operation in an effort to reduce these costs. One of these initiatives became the Clean Development Mechanism.

Since it does not matter where greenhouse gases are emitted, a reduction of emissions anywhere in the world counts. The Clean Development Mechanism allows countries from the South to help Northern countries achieve their targets through the implementation of projects that reduce emissions in Southern countries. This does not exempt the North from reducing emissions at home, as the Clean Development Mechanism stipulates that the majority of its emissions must be achieved through domestic action. The incentive to invest in these projects is that the cost of reducing emissions is lowered for the Northern emitters. A condition of the Clean Development Mechanism is that projects must show real, measurable emission reductions and contribute to sustainable development of the Southern host country.

The Clean Development Mechanism is unique, involving as it does a form of trade based on a mutual benefit for richer and poorer countries. For the first time the idea of sustainable development has been set as a pre-condition. Flows of development finance and green technologies will enable the South to leapfrog to cleaner and more sustainable solutions.

The Clean Development Mechanism has been greeted with tremendous excitement, and many have written about the 'Kyoto surprise', a late night gift delivered on the last day of exhausting negotiations in Kyoto in 1997. But the implementation of the Clean Development Mechanism is very challenging and has led to the development of a highly complex instrument.

SouthSouthNorth was set up to take on this challenge and to find answers to the many questions raised by Clean Development Mechanism projects...

What is sustainable development really? **Can one measure it?** How can one ensure that emission reductions are real? How can they be measured? How can one prevent the unscrupulous from cheating the planet for a quick buck? **What attracts Northern finance to good Southern projects?** How can one stimulate an organised, flexible market which drives investment in real reductions? How should projects be managed, structured and designed? **How can we ensure equity in bringing projects to poorer countries where emissions are low so there is little to trade?** How can public and private institutions and individuals identify and use the Clean Development Mechanism to transform business as usual into sustainable development?

CREATING SOUTHSOUTHNORTH

Three friends met at the fifth conference of the parties of the United Nations Framework Convention on Climate Change held in Bonn in 1999. Hélène Connor of Helio International, Steve Thorne, a South African energy consultant, and Emilio La Rovere, a Brazilian professor, presented a paper on 'Criteria and Indicators for Sustainable Development in the Clean Development Mechanism'. With them was a newcomer, Stef Raubenheimer, also from South Africa. Afterwards, in discussions with Paul Hassing of the Department of Foreign Affairs of the Dutch Government, it was agreed to test the ideas put forward in the paper with actual projects in a number of developing countries. This was the origin of SouthSouthNorth.

Stefan Raubenheimer, *Chief Executive Officer of SouthSouthNorth:* At that time I knew nothing about Kyoto. I had been a lawyer involved in conflict resolution in South Africa from 1994 onwards. I had done a lot of mediation around the time of the elections and after that I had spearheaded a new form of third party intervention that we called 'development facilitation'. It was basically the facilitation of sustainable development. Steve knew about my work. I was chatting to him at home and he showed me the two or three paragraphs of article twelve of the Kyoto Protocol. He said 'read this'. I had an instant recognition that this was a very brilliant and unusual idea, this Clean Development Mechanism. And so I said to him 'I want to work in this field. What can I contribute?' Steve said the only people in this field were the scientists and the politicians. 'We need process people.' And deep in that moment we had the beginnings of the idea of marrying technical interventions with process interventions, which is what SouthSouthNorth was soon to be all about. Not long afterward, I was on a plane to Bonn.

When you go to these United Nations conferences they are massively bewildering things, especially if you don't know the area. I hadn't done much reading – I hadn't had time. There were five thousand people all with a role of some sort, all scurrying around, this new language, a new jargon, all this action going on. So for someone who is ignorant it is quite intimidating! I was in Steve's shadow, holding onto his belt following him around. A clipboard carrier. Three days later I had five new friends who had placed their trust in my ability to learn and asked me to be the executive officer of SouthSouthNorth. That was the start of my third career.

Hélène Connor, *Helio International:* I can tell you a little about how SouthSouthNorth came about. I am no longer a teenager and I realised that I wanted to do something very useful if I could. I pulled together all the people in Helio International, a group which I formed to examine energy systems throughout the world. Emilio La Rovere and Steve Thorne were among them. When the climate issue was developing we realised that we did not like too much the Clean Development Mechanism because it was going to be market defined and that it could detract from real efficiency measures and policies which could be conducive for people domestically. We wanted to make sure that the mechanism would be good. At one of our Helio meetings in Cape Town I realised that our methodologies for analysing energy policies could be adapted to evaluate Clean Development Mechanism projects. We were very conscious that if southern countries were not taking their own destinies in hand, it would all happen in the North. So this is how the name came about: first of all South – South exchange of technologies and expertise and then partnerships with the North.

Emilio la Rovere, *Alberto Luiz Coimbra Institute of Post Graduate Studies and Research in Engineering/Federal University of Rio de Janeiro, Brazil:* The Clean Development Mechanism is like a lemon, really like the seed of a lemon. We had to make it grow, to water it, to find the sugar, to make lemonade. To make sure it is not too sour. SouthSouthNorth: that is what we do – we make lemonade. Steve and I presented our paper in Bonn in 1999. Afterwards we discussed the idea of trying to apply the ideas in the paper to real projects. Paul Hassing of the Dutch government showed enthusiasm for this approach. That was exactly when SouthSouthNorth started. The core was to be Brazil and South Africa, because of Steve and myself. Two countries were not enough for testing, so Paul encouraged us to look to Asia. We decided on Bangladesh, as a very poor country, and Indonesia for its size and its level of development.

Atiq Rahman, *Bangladesh Centre for Advanced Studies:* SouthSouthNorth is an excellent initiative, I think first of all the group itself is powerful, effective, key players in the game; it's a combination of the best of the South.

Agus Sari, *Pelangi, Indonesia:* The whole of SouthSouthNorth has become larger than the sum of us.

Steve Thorne, *South Africa:* It's been a wonderful experience, bringing these teams of people, this expertise together. I've got an incredible team here in South Africa; it is growing every day, extending its capacity and confidence.

Hélène Connor-Lajambe, Ph.D., has a long history of environmental activism internationally. She has created a number of international organisations; she heads Helio International and has developed the Sustainable Energy Watch. She holds an M.B.A. and earned a doctorate in Economics. Specialised in energy and sustainable development, she has written extensively on those topics and contributed to debates in the international arena, in particular at the UNCSD and the UNFCCC.

International Monitoring
HELIO

Helio International: With its nodes of independent observers worldwide, Helio International contributes proactively to improving energy sustainability and to solving problems linked to the implementation of eco-development. Its goals are to assess, monitor and publicise the contribution of energy systems to genuine sustainable development. It promotes clean, secure and efficient energy systems by assessing and monitoring the contribution of energy systems to an improved quality of life and to check the implementation of environmental Conventions and principles. Helio's mission is to report its findings to key energy decision-makers and society at large.

Helio International's Monitoring Advisory Committee Members are: José Goldemberg, University of Sao Paulo, Brazil, Axel Michaelowa, Hamburg Institute of International Economics, Germany, Lasse Ringius, UNEP Risoe, Denmark, Liam Salter, WWF Bangkok, Youba Sokona, ENDA-TM Energie, Dakar, Senegal

MAKING THE CLEAN DEVELOPMENT MECHANISM WORK

The Clean Development Mechanism is a brilliant idea, but it raises questions of value and integrity. The mechanism can produce huge volumes of trading with little real emission reduction and zero sustainable development. Or it can produce the sustainable development that SouthSouthNorth hoped it would.

Steve Thorne: The potential for cheating with the Clean Development Mechanism is huge. Both the buyers and the sellers have the same interests, which is to inflate the whole level of emission reductions. That is why there have to be rules to ensure that the emissions are real. Stringency has been fundamental to our approach to finding a way in which the global intention can be properly administered. We are looking at the same time at the shift between what is sustainable development and what is business as usual. We are saying this is the way things were done before and this is the way they could be done in the future. The reason that we are pushing sustainable development around global emissions is precisely because it has not been part of the development paradigm before. This is the thin edge of the wedge. If we don't get it right now we won't find a way of dealing with sustainable development with multi-lateral agreements in the future.

Emilio La Rovere: First think about development, then think about mitigating climate change as a natural unfolding of sustainable development.

Atiq Rahman: My fundamental concern is that the Clean Development Mechanism is morally wrong. It is trying to transfer the responsibility of the competent, the doers, to the less competent, less able societies. It is transferring the solution of the problem to those who have not created the problem. The whole question is based on the concept of economic efficiency. If it is more efficient to do it in a poorer country then the whole idea of development has to be much more socially oriented. Let's go back to the fundamental issue: the capacity building needed in the South to make the mechanism more responsive to sustainable development. The requirement of sustainable development, the human quality in this, the societal needs, bringing the victims' voices into the equation: that is the real challenge. We in SouthSouthNorth believe in that and that it can be done.

Agus Sari: What appealed to me about SouthSouthNorth is that we start very much from the development point of view. This is the start of a culture of co-operation between the North and the South; among those who are affected by climate change – those who are sceptical or optimistic about the future of a 'climate regime'. We want to make sure that global benefit is not produced at the expense of local sustainability.

Stefan Raubenheimer: SouthSouthNorth is built on a value system. It is all about learning, getting a great number of people into a learning network to share these values about development, making this work in a professional way, and opening the market to really make a difference. Implementing the Clean Development Mechanism is highly complicated, time consuming and expensive. There is very little expertise internationally, especially in countries of the South. SouthSouthNorth is committed to the success of this mechanism and to sustainable development, to protect the environment, to alleviate poverty, and to achieve equity and social justice.

Hélène Connor: The Clean Development Mechanism was constructed around a North/South axis. SouthSouthNorth is an interesting name: now in all the texts you can see South – South exchange popping up. It has brought about a new consciousness in people. This is SouthSouthNorth's force: to bring people into the network to ask themselves questions.

THE SOUTHSOUTHNORTH PROJECT RECIPE

SouthSouthNorth creates a partnership with a project developer and forms a project development team. This team comprises multiple parties – lawyers, bankers, scientists, engineers, community leaders, anthropologists and is led by SouthSouthNorth trained project facilitators. Together they craft the project, testing its feasibility and ensuring its contribution to sustainable development against the SouthSouthNorth Matrix Tool.

The technical co-ordinators initiate a regular peer review of both the sustainability appraisal and the project design.

Monitors from Helio International oversee the process to ensure transparency and stringency.

The project design document emerges from this process, which is the blue print for the Clean Development Mechanism.

The central office creates information and technology links to support and coordinate the output of the four country teams. It ensures that open channels of communication are maintained within the network itself and with other countries of the south and of the north. This enable a synergistic exchange both of information and of technology for the benefit of global capacity building.

11

BRAZIL
accounting for technology

Technology must start with the context if you are to arrive at technology that meets your needs. Many projects first address the technology and then the context. That is the way that technology flows from the North to the South: technologies are conceived for Northern countries and dumped in the South. We are trying to do things the other way around by starting with the context. That is the concept of appropriate technology.

Emilio La Rovere, *Team Leader SouthSouthNorth, Brazil*

13

BRAZIL'S continental vastness is mirrored in the economic distances between its richest and poorest citizens. The Amazon basin, the great, green lung of our planet, lies at its centre, far from the huge cities along the Atlantic coastline and the political capital, Brasilia. Portuguese stitches together one hundred and seventy two million people, fashioning a common national identity that enables Brazilians to think across these spaces. It is also the thread that weaves together into one all the cultures of Brazil: the original inhabitants, descendents of African slaves transported in great numbers for four hundred years, and Europeans. The varied faces of Brazil's people bear witness to more than five hundred years of enterprise and violence that has left a legacy of great wealth and extreme poverty.

Rio de Janeiro, where the SouthSouthNorth team in Brazil is based, is a juxtaposition of the extravagance of Copacabana, undulating around a golden ribbon of beach, and the favelas that cling to sheer cliffs and then flatten out into the horizon.

With its edgy elegance and its desperation, Rio encapsulates the paradox and challenges of a world simultaneously so rich and so poor. This challenge has been taken up by the SouthSouthNorth team, based at the Federal University of Brazil, where the focus has been promoting sustainable development through Brazilian-based technological innovation. The conviction that renewable energy needs champions is central to Brazil's technically complex, experimental projects. The link between these projects is the determination to maximise the huge potential of waste, a metastasising global problem, as a renewable energy source.

Thus Brazil is the technical laboratory of SouthSouthNorth. The team navigates between a highly developed economy and a scavenging economy, tapping into the former to develop imaginative technology that will contribute towards dealing with an urgent social agenda. One project is testing ways of converting used cooking oil from a fast food chain into bio-diesel to fuel the garbage trucks that ferry and dump the city's garbage. A second project deals with bio-gas extracted from Rio's landfill, generating electricity for operating the landfill. A third project is piloting a technologically innovative power plant fuelled by solid waste. These projects lend themselves to replication across Brazil, and have the potential to re-orientate development in the South. SouthSouthNorth in Brazil is thus accounting for technology as a lever for development and as a way to reduce poverty.

VOICES FROM BRAZIL

Paulo Jardim, *Technical Co-ordinator, COMLURB:* These projects are about how to make the Clean Development Mechanism feasible and practical. They deal with climate change in a realistic way. We are helping alleviate environmental problems and producing 'green' electricity. I would like to see renewable energies and a clean environment in the future. This will really be useful for everyone in the world, not only for you and your children. We can provide good examples for others about how to live in harmony with nature.

Fernando Sandroni, *Usinaverde:* The aim is to generate electricity from garbage, to solve the ecological problems. We are looking for technology that can deal with our ecological problem in an economically friendly way.

The aim is to generate electricity from garbage, to solve the ecological problems.

Luciano Oliveira, *Technical Co-ordinator, SouthSouthNorth:*
The most difficult challenge is for the Brazilian government to develop an official position about emissions and the Clean Development Mechanism. Once the Kyoto Protocol is enforced things will be clearer and we will move ahead more quickly.

Alexandre Davignon, *Development Facilitator, SouthSouthNorth:* The partnership with other countries in SouthSouthNorth enriches our work. We know these environmental problems are shared by most developing countries, which helps us join together to find solutions to most problems. There is no area in our work where we didn't learn because in these projects you have all the environmental aspects: local, regional and global.

EMILIO LA ROVERE
Team Leader, SouthSouthNorth, Brazil

We looked at where you could reduce emissions in a given area by using different technology.

SouthSouthNorth is a journey: We did not know what would happen, what would come from this adventure of identifying projects and putting them to work, because the Clean Development Mechanism was still a very new issue. This is exactly what we mean by learning by doing. Here in Brazil we are already seen as pioneers.

In Brazil a lot of effort was put into renewable energy in the 1970s because we were a large oil importer. A number of technologies were developed but most of them were not commercially viable and in 1986, when the oil price dropped, they were put aside. When you do find a niche where the technology can be competitive, especially if you can get the help of carbon certificates, then only can you make use of these innovations. We first look at our context, the sector, the emissions, what we have, what we know about, and we work things out from there.

At first we had only the bare terms of the Clean Development Mechanism, but in order to make it work optimally, and in order to test a given project, we designed a methodology and a screening process for selecting projects. We had a number of criteria against which to check project concepts. We started with project indicators: a set of indicators to check the desirability of the project in terms of sustainable development. There is another set of indicators to check the feasibility of the project. We looked at where you could reduce emissions in a given area by using different technology. You might think you have the final solution to all the problems of mankind but you have to see if implementation is possible. You need to evaluate the risk and you need a reasonable probability of success.

We ended up with thirty two projects that could be used to reduce emissions. Then we screened these projects with our development indicators, which is how we settled on these few projects in Brazil. And this was the purpose of the project: to check that our methodology was designed appropriately. We have been very conservative. The projects do not have much social impact at this stage but they do well in other aspects. We picked up on projects that are not very big solutions in themselves but are projects that you can replicate. If a fast food chain can recycle its used oil as a fuel – this can be replicated and amplified later. On a larger scale of course it will create jobs, which has clear social benefits.

You need a risk taker to champion these projects. You could call it an entrepreneurial capacity – a capacity to innovate. You can't succeed without someone who believes in the project and pushes it, almost as a matter of faith. Not having someone who is really convinced and who wants to convince everybody of his projects can be an institutional hurdle. It is perhaps the most difficult barrier for renewable energy.

Here in Brazil we are already seen as pioneers.

Emilio Lèbre La Rovere's background is in systems engineering and economics. He has an M.Sc. in Systems Engineering from COPPE/UFRJ and a Ph.D. in Economics from the School of Higher Studies in Social Sciences, University of Paris. He is currently Professor of the Energy Planning Program at COPPE/UFRj and Co-ordinator of the Environmental Sciences Laboratory and the Centre for Integrated Studies on Climate Change and the Environment at COPPE/UFRJ. He was the head of department in 1995-1996 and of the M.Sc. /Ph.D. Environmental Planning Course from 1988 to 1997. He worked in the Agency for Financing Studies, Research and Development Projects of the Brazilian Federal Government (1975 to 1988). He has consulted for numerous international agencies. He is Lead Author of the Intergovernmental Panel on Climate Change, Second Assessment Report (SAR), Working Group III, chapters 8 and 9; of the IPCC Special Report on Emissions Scenarios; and of chapter 2 of WG III of the Third Assessment Report (TAR); Co-ordinating Lead Author of chapter 3 of WG II of TAR; and author of several reports prepared for the Secretariat of the United Nations Framework Convention on Climate Change.

FLAVIA NADALUTTI & ALEXANDRE DAVIGNON
Development Facilitators, SouthSouthNorth, Brazil

It is not the technology of a machine. It is knowledge: the technology of the mind.

SouthSouthNorth is an experience – one that can be written for the world so that they can learn from this initiative. We have three things to share with the rest of the world: innovation, new technologies, and the knowledge to replicate these. Testing the technology is important. It is not exactly the technology of a machine – it is the knowledge of how to apply or transfer technology. People can produce energy from the natural resources that we have in Brazil, so we can implement projects here that will contribute to cleaning the atmosphere.

When I first read about the Clean Development Mechanism I asked myself how I could do this. But we are learning by implementing it. Everybody needs to learn and our research in Brazil is innovative. We can now explain to people how to create and implement projects in the private market that bring real and sustainable benefits. We worked closely with project owners who are very committed to the projects. With the private company, Hidroveg, that produces the bio-diesel everything happened very fast. On the other hand, the city utility that manages the landfill is partly public and partly private, so the rhythm is a little different and it took longer to explain the process to the board and the president.

We have also made contacts with the other countries. I like that we can collaborate and work locally and globally. It is a very interesting model. The environment is so critical. It is vital for us to develop such projects, to communicate with people, to develop a sound methodology, to be involved in global, not just local efforts.

What is really important is that we are helping and participating in a project that contributes to the mitigation of greenhouse gases. The project owners like this aspect. They are keen to receive carbon credits for implementing their projects correctly and for contributing to sustainable development. The companies see the money – the lucre – of course. But it is an exchange: you give me this, I give you that. It allows you to balance interests that are usually opposed.

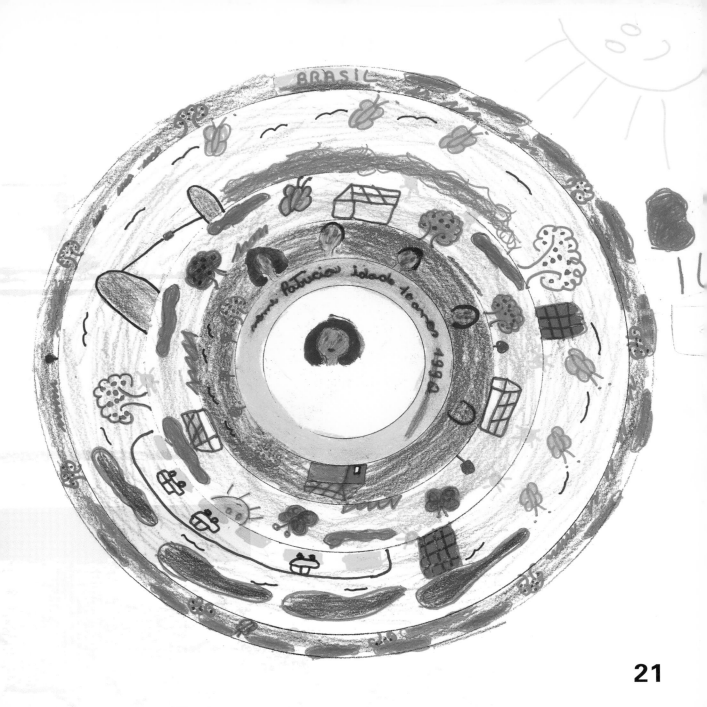

21

ELECTRICITY GENERATION
FROM BIO-GAS AND BIO-DIESEL

Projected savings: 35 000 tons of carbon dioxide over ten years

The Jardim Gramacho Landfill at Duque de Caxias, Rio de Janeiro, illustrates the potential for generating electricity from renewable energy sources, such as bio-gas, produced from the decomposition of organic solid wastes in landfills, and bio-diesel, produced from used vegetable (cooking) oils.

A power generator driven by bio-fuel has been installed at the Jardim Gramacho Landfill, which will ensure at least partial energy self-sufficiency for the operation of the landfill site. The electricity currently bought from the national grid will be replaced by electricity produced by the power generator at the landfill, fuelled by seventy percent bio-diesel and thirty percent bio-gas, both renewable fuels. Through the power generation process methane will be converted into carbon dioxide, reducing the greenhouse gas effect twenty one-fold. The project is owned by the Rio de Janeiro Urban Cleaning Company (COMLURB). Hidroveg Industrias Quimicas Ltd will provide the bio-diesel. It is projected that this project will reduce emissions by thirty five thousand tons over a ten year period.

Rachel Henriques, *Technical Assistant. SouthSouthNorth:* Garbage is a huge problem and it will only get worse if we don't search for solutions right now. Anything you do helps. Ten million people in Rio produce eight thousand tons a day. We don't have enough space. The emissions are also dangerous for global warming, and can be very dangerous at the landfill. This project extracts methane gas from the landfill and bio-diesel made from used oil and uses them to generate power.

Luciana La Paz, *Technical Assistant. SouthSouthNorth:* People will act if you offer an economic benefit. I don't know if we will really change their minds about what is important for the global environment: our projects offer economical solutions. We have to link the environmental questions to economic incentives if we are to achieve global health.

Paulo Roberto Jardim, *Technical Co-ordinator. COMLURB:* Learning about the mechanism of the Kyoto Protocol is very important in the technological development and the environmental protection, for COMLURB and for the mayor of the city. If we did not have this channel then maybe we would not have started this project. Without SouthSouthNorth it would have taken much longer. It is very easy to work with them – that is the good thing. We have a common goal to solve our problems. We have to solve global problems – that is our ultimate objective. But we have practical problems at the Gramacho Landfill. One is to make the wells produce bio-gas of high enough quality. You have to control the use of bio-diesel and bio-gas in the right proportion to provide the output we need to feed the generator.

We have not solved all the technical problems yet, but we are working to solve them and we are all very proud of the Gramacho Landfill. The Clean Development Mechanism makes it easier to convince the company directors about the project. Not to use the gas is illogical.

PROJECT PARTICIPANT

Penido Monteiro, *COMLURB:* I always thought of a landfill as a kind of petroleum well. I could not accept that we, a poor country as Brazil is, never utilised this potential as a combustible. This can be very helpful for small cities also. I really believe that this project – this small pilot project – can be replicated in many other cities in the country.

As a city we committed a tremendous crime against the environment. I knew Gramacho when it was a mangrove swamp - it was beautiful, marvellous ...

In 1995, after twenty years of bad practice, COMLURB started to recover the landfill. This decision was made with the election of the current mayor in 1993, and the new board of directors. They said we have to close the site. We, the technicians, said close Gramacho and put the garbage where? It is not so simple. Some months later we finally convinced the directors not to close Gramacho but to recover it and operate it as a sanitary landfill. The board was convinced and they convinced the mayor. We decided to design a plant for energy generation with SouthSouthNorth. We wanted to do something with the gas,

As a city we committed a tremendous crime against the environment. I knew Gramacho when it was a mangrove swamp – it was beautiful, marvellous ... But eight years ago it was an open dump, horrible.

But eight years ago it was an open dump, horrible. There were fires all around; the liquid pollution went straight into the bay. All the mangroves were completely destroyed. Jardim Gramacho was designed to be a sanitary landfill. There was an agreement that each municipality should pay something for the running of the landfill. But nobody ever paid, the money disappeared and the supposed sanitary landfill turned into a horrible open dump and destroyed about one million square metres of mangrove, a site protected by our state constitution.

All of the problems related to waste management in Brazil are the responsibility of the municipalities, so it always depends on a political decision of the mayor.

not just waste it. This is an experimental pilot project and we can see all the problems, but it is very interesting technology. The municipalities are very poor and landfills are the last priorities of the mayor. Carbon credits can really help with the recovery of what we have all around Brazil – open horrible dump sites – and their conversion into sanitary landfills.

25

Waste pickers waiting,
Gramacho Landfill

PROJECT BENEFICIARIES

Luciana la Paz, *SouthSouthNorth:* Many people live off the garbage. The people who go there to pick through the garbage are just poor people so you can just close your eyes to it.

Paulo Jardim: You cannot force people to change, force the scavengers away. That is not the way – they just come back. These people come from all over the area. They make two or three hundred a month: equal to two minimum wages a month. It is not ideal but it is a means of living. So there are social and economic problems involved that are beyond the engineering. We are trying to move them to a smaller plant to recycle there. But people say they earn more money picking the waste. Some of them prefer it to working in a plant like a factory worker, which some of them are not used to doing. They are more like freelancers. Yes, some of them see themselves as small entrepreneurs.

Flavia Nadalutti: Energy is becoming increasingly expensive in Brazil. So if you can extract the bio-gas and use it to generate electricity it saves money for other things: perhaps to pay for the recycling factory, to create more jobs, to pay for the landfill. We are concerned about the social benefits. The president of the association of the scavengers wrote to us. They make their living by recycling. He understands that the implementation of this project will be a benefit to the atmosphere and he hopes for them also. He knew about the project because they are one of the stakeholders that are directly involved. They were of course worried about their work. The scavengers want to continue with their work – picking through the garbage and recycling.

27

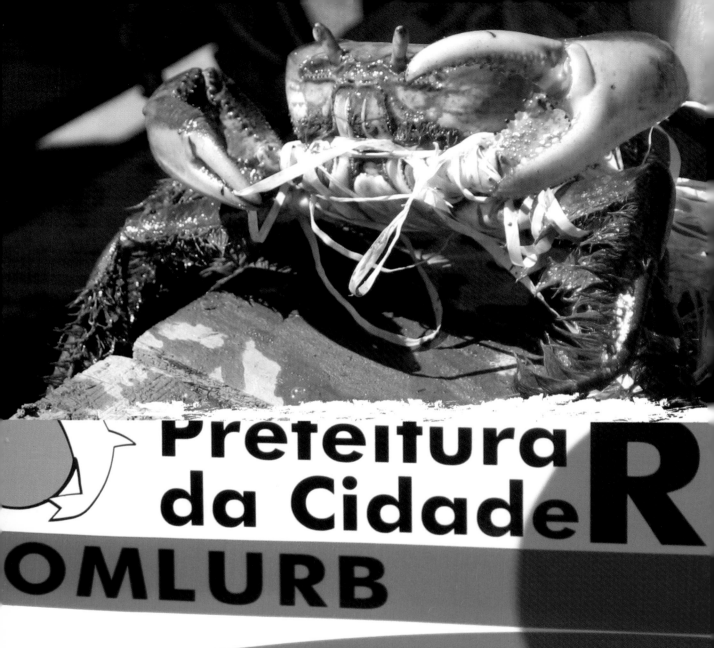

Prefeitura da Cidade R

OMLURB

28

RIO SEM ARMAS

The electricity generated at the plant is used to clean the water produced at the landfill site. Dangerous chemicals like ammonia are extracted so that only clean water is returned to Guanabara Bay. This has led to the rehabilitation of a great swathe of mangrove swamp. This acts as a 'biological monitor': as soon as any poisons escape the landfill the trees burn and the problem can be resolved at once. Birds, fish and animals like crabs are returning to the mangrove swamp and making it their home again.

29

BIO-DIESEL FOR THE TRANSPORT SECTOR

Projected savings: 38 500 tons of carbon dioxide over ten years

31

This project aims to partially replace diesel, a fossil fuel, with bio-diesel in the transport sector. Bio-diesel is made by submitting vegetable oil to a chemical process called transesterisation. The beauty of bio-diesel is that it can be used in an ordinary diesel engine.

The project owner is Hidroveg Industrias Quimica Ltda, an innovative company that runs a bio-diesel processing plant in Rio de Janeiro. The McDonald's fast food chain contributes used cooking oil which, instead of being dumped, is being converted to bio-diesel as part of this pilot project. The bio-diesel that is produced by this project will fuel two of the Rio de Janeiro Urban Cleaning Company (COMLURB) garbage trucks and Hidroveg's fleet, both of which currently use diesel. Replacing the non-renewable carbon dioxide emitting cycle (diesel) with a renewable carbon dioxide emitting cycle (bio-diesel) will reduce emissions of carbon dioxide by thirty eight and a half thousand tons over a ten year period.

Rachel Henriques, Luciana La Paz, Luciano Oliveira, *SouthSouthNorth:* Brazil currently imports forty percent of its diesel. Because you can use bio-diesel in an ordinary diesel engine, we can substitute this with bio-diesel which emits less greenhouse gas. With bio-diesel you have a closed system because growing plants absorb carbon dioxide; then you take the seed, extract the oil and use it. What you are using has already extracted carbon dioxide from the atmosphere.

This is a very important new step and we are piloting the technology with used cooking oil to produce bio-diesel. McDonalds in Brazil want to do this as part of their social marketing. There are fifty McDonalds in Rio that can provide used oil to Hidroveg to make bio-diesel. We negotiated a ten year contract with McDonalds so they will supply us with the oil free of charge.

Hidroveg makes bio-diesel – they are responsible for over seventy percent of the local market. Bio-diesel is a new market that is opening and if Hidroveg has the technology to do this then they can expand into other markets. These are very important opportunities for Hidroveg.

Rachel Henriques: You can build complex projects to include many goals starting with the technology of bio-diesel and then reaching wider into the social realm. This will help with the decentralisation of energy. There are many aspects to it. You are helping people who are planting these plants: people will have work if they collect the plants for the oil. Our expectation is also that we can export this product. We have lots of natural palm trees in Amazonia. We just need to collect the fruit – it is an opportunity to maintain isolated communities in economic terms and it can help stop deforestation. One of the reasons for deforestation is that these small communities don't have the means to survive. If you offer them a way to survive economically without deforestation they will do it.

Luciano Oliveira, *Technical Co-ordinator for Projects, SouthSouthNorth:* Many small towns and communities generate electricity from diesel. People use generators in small communities and towns in the whole of Amazonia. It makes the project easier to replicate if you have bio-diesel. People know how it works – you don't have to have special engines or specially trained people because everyone already knows how to fix the diesel engines.

PROJECT PARTICIPANT

Antonio Lamon, *Industrial Director, Hidroveg:* I am interested in this bio-diesel project and the carbon credits because I have specialised in agriculture and also I am an entrepreneur. Hidroveg specialises in the production of fuels and chemicals from agricultural products. I want to produce things that can work to maximise the possibilities for Brazil. Bio-diesel has huge scope here in Brazil because of our agricultural potential and the fact that you can grow almost anything here. I am also a nationalist. Bio-diesel will help Brazil against petroleum price fluctuations – it is a very strategic project.

Collecting used oil,
Rio de Janeiro

33

ELECTRICITY GENERATION FROM **SOLID WASTE**

Projected savings: 365 000 tons of carbon dioxide over ten years

35

Unknown Brazil

Known Brazil...
Is the one that has hunger
It is Brazil of poverty and misery

Unknown Brazil...
It is the Brazil that hopes for a better day

Known Brazil...
For violence, for lost bullets
killing the innocent
Even inside the schools

Unknown Brazil...
It is the Brazil of solidarity,
Of volunteers for peace
Known Brazil...
It is the people of empty pots
It is the life of a poor people
Without hope of better days

Unknown Brazil...
Of people watching the sun set
on the summer evenings at the beach
Besides their beloved

Known Brazil...
It is of revenge, of hate and
without love
With sex without passion

Unknown Brazil...
Belongs to romantics
To divinations of skin and saliva,
To tears, clouds, quindim, breezes and
philosophy;
To flirts, scoundrels, schemes and
Even passion insane

If you haven't discovered Brazil
It is because you haven't yet gone mad
That necessary little bit
To bring life to a halt and see
Where it doesn't make any sense.
Unravel

José Lima Wilson Lima da Rocha
Favela resident, 18 years old
Rio de Janeiro

36

This project at the Ilha do Fundão Campus of the Federal University of Rio de Janeiro involves the construction of a power plant to be fuelled by urban solid. The project participants are COMLURB and Usinaverde, a private company whose aim is to generate electricity from garbage.

The benefits are generating electricity for the campus and reducing the garbage that the University must send to sanitary landfills. The proposed plant can take thirty tons of garbage a day and has the potential to produce one megawatt of electricity once the project is implemented. Since this is a pilot project within a research centre, there will be systems to monitor all aspects of the plant. The total avoided emissions are three hundred and sixty five thousand tons of carbon dioxide over a period of ten years

PROJECT OWNER

Fernando Sandroni, USINAVERDE: This is a pilot plant. We will collect waste mainly from the university, but also from the surrounding areas if it is needed. It is not difficult – it is a very clear and simple project. The starting point is that there is a world-wide problem with waste. But we must deal with the problem in Brazil which is a developing country. We cannot anymore use solutions that do not take care of the ecological aspects – the air, the water, our surroundings. On the other hand we cannot afford the huge investments they can in the developed world. We are searching for a solution that is acceptable and where the investments are not so big. So we have developed an appropriate technology and we are piloting this new technology in our new plant. We believe that the costs of this plant will be much lower than those being used in developed countries.

It is still a prototype but to build bigger plants we will need investors: we cannot do it with our own resources. This environmentally friendly and appropriate technology is most suitable for the Clean Development Mechanism. First you do not destroy everything – you recycle the glass. The waste that is left is turned into electric energy. The only thing over is salt that can be used for agriculture. It is a closed situation so you can establish such a plant near the cities. This will lower the cost of disposal and there will be much less diesel burnt into the atmosphere by transporting garbage to distant dump sites. We would make our money by being contracted by municipalities to get rid of their garbage. It is magic – I always ask what is wrong here. There must be something wrong. It is too perfect.

SouthSouthNorth is using this project as a Clean Development Mechanism example. The potential in this for carbon trading will be a major factor in the environmental and economic viability of this project.

37

RICARDO CUNHA DA COSTA & MAURO ARAUJO ALMEIDA
The Helio Monitors, Brazil

Monitors help to ensure effectiveness, efficiency, relevance and sustainability of projects. They ensure accountability based on transparent procedures. Their comprehensive assessment of the projects develops monitoring skills and feeds back the results and lessons learned.

There is a lot of specificity in the SouthSouthNorth projects in Brazil. We tried to understand the details and then we tried to produce a dedicated way of monitoring them. We are working with very skilled people who know how to implement projects. The SouthSouthNorth projects have a lot of potential for industry in Brazil. There are also social benefits – especially in bio-fuels. One of the problems with deforestation in the Amazon is that people don't earn enough money to stay where they are – people go into the forest and take away resources. After a short time they have to move because there is nothing left. Activities that will put money into these regions are important as they will bring employment, develop a national technology and reduce environmental damage.

The first work we did was to try to understand how the SouthSouthNorth team developed the projects. We worked closely with them and discussed how to do the work. I think they are very capable and understand these kinds of projects. And we learned these things with them. But when we disagreed on some things they are there to explain and to try and convince us. We have always managed to reach a compromise although we have seen some estimates differently to them. For instance, they considered the biomass from a landfill as a renewable resource. Some methods consider it renewable but others do not, so we checked on this and discussed it. They needed to convince us that they are right. I think that it is because it is all so new. We must work out how things should be done.

We are almost like detectives. We have to check it all. They make estimates and we try to verify if these are real or not. Afterwards they can revise things. They can do it better the next time.

Ricardo Cunha da Costa, PhD, is research fellow at the Energy Planning Program of the Federal University of Rio de Janeiro and an associated researcher at the Centre for Integrated Studies on Climate Change and the Environment (Centro Clima). He is interested in energy-economy models and climate change.

Mauro Araujo Almeida is a Mechanical Engineer, Ph.D. graduated in the Energy Planning Program the Federal University of Rio de Janeiro. He is a researcher of Centre for Integrated Studies on Climate Change and the Environment, where he works with the monitoring of Clean Development Mechanism projects.

39

BANGLADESH
accounting for poverty

The fundamental question is poverty and development. There are very few
people who see beyond Bangladesh's poverty to the vibrancy and enterprise
of its people. We say every human being has one mouth, two hands. If you
enable the hands to produce, then feeding the mouth is no problem.

Atiq Rahman, *Team Leader SouthSouthNorth, Bangladesh*

BANGLADESH is a huge delta: the three great rivers that drain the Indian sub-continent flow through Bangladesh and into the Bay of Bengal. It is at once an intricate web of waterways and a potential disaster zone when the monsoon sweeps through each year. The countryside is an iridescent tapestry of paddy fields, rivers and bamboo houses precariously perched on stilts. And people everywhere – working, talking, walking, cooking – every available inch of land is cultivated. Less than one hundred and fifty thousand square kilometres has to feed a population of more than one hundred and thirty three million people, a quarter of whom are now crammed into cities like Dhaka and Chittagong.

The enormous population of Bangladesh places unbearable pressure on this fragile and profligately fertile ecosystem. Bangladesh is one of the poorest countries on earth, but the exuberance and enterprise of its people contests the 'basket case' image bequeathed to it.

Bangladeshis consume very little energy – only eighteen per cent of households are connected to the electricity grid. Greenhouse gas emissions are negligible: a fifth of a ton of carbon dioxide emissions per capita per year, compared to nearly twenty tons per capita annually in the United States. In Bangladesh there is less than one car per one thousand people, whereas in the United States there are four hundred and seventy five cars for every thousand. Because emissions in Bangladesh are negligible, it has almost nothing to trade. This makes it very difficult for Bangladesh, like other very poor and undeveloped countries, to leverage investment through the Clean Development Mechanism. Carbon revenues will remain elusive as they have so few emissions to reduce and therefore almost nothing to sell. This is the paradoxical heart of the Clean Development Mechanism. How does one make this mechanism work for the poorest Southern countries, like Bangladesh, which have not been drawn into the ambit of global development?

The SouthSouthNorth team in Bangladesh have chosen challenging projects – Solar Home Systems in isolated rural areas and electric vehicles in Dhaka City – that push the definition of what Clean Development projects can be, of what the Clean Development Mechanism itself is. They are a valuable case study for integrating non-industrialised countries into a sustainable future and ensuring that the global community accounts for poverty.

VOICES FROM BANGLADESH

Mahfuzul Haque, *Deputy Secretary. Ministry of Environment and Forestry:* Climate change is an issue that is very important in Bangladesh. If there's a one metre sea level rise, a large portion of Bangladesh will go under water. But changes are taking place because people are very conscious. That awareness comes from education, the media and globalisation. To cut a tree or not: that is a million dollar question these days. You cannot cut a tree down here: people will gather and they will stop you doing that. There is great amount of awareness among the people especially the younger generation, that's a good thing. That is my special capital. Built on that capital I'm sure we have something to look forward to for the future in Bangladesh.

In earlier days it was evenly distributed in the western area. The land is also getting drier and drier. Changes in climate put additional stress on the ratio of space allocated under normal circumstances to marginal farmers. It also threatens what remains of natural habitat where turtles and dolphins live in the water, and birds and animals on the land.

Atiq Rahman, *Team Leader SouthSouthNorth:* Our vision for the future is to ensure food security, energy security and water security for each citizen.

Around 42% of the population of Bangladesh are living below the poverty line. This is one of the major factors of social vulnerability.

Moinul Islam Sharif, *SouthSouthNorth:* People are realising that something is changing in the weather. But what it is they don't understand. They don't know the longer term implications of climate change.

Scientists can relate things to global warming. The rural people really don't know what climate change is, but they understand that something is going wrong. The monsoon rain is not really happening the way it should. Now during the monsoon we are observing a very intense rainfall within a short period of time.

45

ATIQ RAHMAN
Team Leader, SouthSouthNorth, Bangladesh

The fundamental question is poverty and development.

I had always been interested in development. I asked myself what am I doing teaching in the United Kingdom? I was very involved in the industrial processes and developing new materials then. I asked myself what is the utility of this for the bottom three quarters of the world's population? The benefit won't reach that population for fifty years! So I said I don't have that much patience, I want them to have some use of the little I have learnt, in the lifetime that I have.

Bangladesh is a small country; we are privileged to be involved in the SouthSouthNorth initiative. The other three are fairly large countries with large economies, so we are like the little one there. But because of the quality of our work and the intellectual competence of our voice, we are able to contribute and to learn. It is a long term learning process that has enabled a number of younger colleagues to be able to take over in the future, because my time will be running out pretty fast. It gives us the opportunity for capacity and institution building. We also address common questions not only among poor countries but in regard to much larger issues. So from quite a small point you radiate out and work.

What we do is social capitalisation. We work with entrepreneurs in Bangladesh and we bring the social capital. Together this makes the commercial input better. Once these pilots start then the commercial world will come in more and more, bringing the fringe benefits. But the system has to be created. The government will not be enthusiastic without good examples so we've brought the good ones forward to set up the examples, to use this process to set the standards to prompt and help set up the government processes.

Atiq Rahman is the Executive Director
of the Bangladesh Centre for Advanced
Studies. He is a leading negotiator in
the international climate change regime
from the South, a co-ordinator of the
North-South Dialogue on Climate Change
and convenor of Climate Action Network
South Asia. He also coordinates the Global
Forum on Environment and Poverty. He
is elected Chairperson of the Coalition
of Environmental non-governmental
organisations, Bangladesh, and continues
to represent this vibrant community
as its principal decision maker. He is
currently Chairman of the Steering
Committee of Asia-Pacific National
Councils for Sustainable Development
whose Secretariat is in Manila. He is also
the Bangladesh Focal Point of the South
Asian Poverty Commission for follow up
action. Besides his work in Bangladesh
and Asia, Dr Rahman has been a Research
Associate at Fletcher School of Law and
Diplomacy, Tuft University, Boston, USA
since 1996. He was also a Faculty Member
of the International Programme on the
Management of Sustainability for the
Sustainability Challenge Foundation in the
Netherlands. He designed, developed and
teaches a multi-disciplinary post-graduate
course on 'Sustainable Development
Challenges and North South Dialogue' at
Massachusetts Institute of Technology,
Department of Urban Studies and Planning,
Cambridge, USA. He is also a Reviewer
of the World Energy Assessment by
the World Energy Council, UNDP and
UNEP and a leading author of the South
Asian intergovernmental policy paper
for the World Summit on Sustainable
Development.

47

MOZAHARUL ALAM (known as Babu)
SouthSouthNorth

We must ensure that the developed world doesn't shift the global responsibility for the environment to the South.

I was interested in the SouthSouthNorth project when I first saw the proposals. It was familiar: greenhouse gas mitigation, what kind of technology you can use. So I committed myself to give my input to the rest. We had our first meeting in The Hague. I had heard about Emilio La Rovere because I had read some of his articles about adaptation. I had met Agus Sari before. The new personalities were Stefan Raubenheimer and Steve Thorne. I first met with Stefan in The Netherlands. He just walked into my apartment and we introduced ourselves. Then he explained the entire project, what to do, what not to do, our programme for the sixth Conference of the Parties.

It is difficult to deal with sustainable development; the market prefers to deal with greenhouse gases: the cost, the price.

It is difficult to deal with sustainable development; the market prefers to deal with greenhouse gases: the cost, the price. The market may not be willing to pay, as there is no international pressure and there is no premium for sustainable development. When we started working with the SouthSouthNorth projects, when we started turning to the nitty gritty of sustainable development and the market mechanism, we found it very difficult. With the market mechanism it is very difficult to ensure the sustainable development of developing countries. When you are putting a price on the emission reduction and you are justifying the sustainable development, in a qualitative manner it is very difficult to measure the two equally.

no rubbish all over
where there were lots of
... of ... they
... traffic jam

49

50

SOLAR HOME SYSTEMS

Projected savings: 8 600 tons of carbon dioxide annually

51

The Solar Home Systems Project aims to provide electricity in isolated areas where grid electricity is not available.

The plan is to install thirty thousand Solar Home Systems over five years. The Solar Home System provides a household with a minimum of two lights and a plug. Having a plug means that it is possible to use a television, a radio, a sewing machine or a fan. The project owner is Grameen Shakti, a renewable energy subsidiary of the internationally respected micro-credit lending agency, Grameen Bank. Rural households not connected to the grid currently use kerosene for lighting and acid leaded batteries to operate televisions. These batteries are usually charged in the nearest marketplace using grid electricity. The Solar Home System will replace these existing sources of energy saving eight thousand six hundred tons of carbon dioxide each year.

Only 18% of the population in Bangladesh is connected to the grid.

Bangladesh has very little to trade at present because emissions are so low. How does it find a niche in the global carbon credit market and convince the private sector to trade?

Atiq Rahman: The Grameen Bank embodies in itself a global image of bringing the poor, particularly women, out of destitution. Grameen Bank brings with them credit and a proven backup system. Grameen and SouthSouthNorth are a very good fit, they're enthusiastic, they're working, and they've understood what we're about, which is sometimes difficult to explain to the ordinary businessman.

Babu: In more industrialised countries, like India, you can have a project which is very good and cost effective but it is not so easy for less industrialised, less polluting countries like Bangladesh. The level of emission from Bangladesh is so low that the amount of money for the reduction will be small. But the management costs of that Clean Development Mechanism project remain the same. To manage a single industry is much less costly than to manage a project that will supply thirty thousand solar home systems. But we are going down this path because we believe that sustainable development should be ensured in the Clean Development Mechanism. We have chosen the two projects so that we can ensure the promotion of the sustainability for Bangladesh.

Moinul Islam Sharif, *SouthSouthNorth:* Only eighteen per cent of the population in Bangladesh is connected to the grid and the possibility of further connection is very unlikely, very slow. And grid electricity will never go to the river islands, or if it does it will take thirty years or more. There is little money available for expansion of electricity for everybody. So we are trying to extract this extra money from the Clean Development Mechanism to make this solar home system more viable for poorer people, to penetrate the poorest levels of society. If we get ten dollars per ton for each carbon credit then the price is twenty percent cheaper. As soon as a household gets a solar

home system the income goes up. There are whole villages electrified by solar power so they can work at night. The women have started working at night – they take up stitching jobs. People can have a fan and a TV – people have information and entertainment. Even the poor people buy a television set. Education levels go up because children can study at night. So the social and financial capital increases.

Khandakar Mainuddin, *SouthSouthNorth:* We worked with the project owners and developed a comprehensive idea of how the Clean Development Mechanism could work and how it would affect the beneficiaries. This is unique in Bangladesh, where there is not much interaction between research and business. So this is a bridge between business and implementation. This kind of thing has not happened before. I had the perception that people might not be very happy with solar energy.

But in a survey we did find that people were willing, that they were very happy to take solar power. Kerosene is messy and you have to travel far to get it. If you have solar power you have more control. I found people in villages who even though they had grid electricity still bought solar systems because of the blackouts.

53

PROJECT PARTICIPANT

Grameen Shakti, the project developer and the executing agency of the project, is one of the family of Grameen companies. It promotes and provides renewable energy resources to the rural areas of Bangladesh. Grameen Shakti provides Solar Home Systems through micro-credit. They are supported by an extensive network of offices sited in the countryside. About eighty percent of Bangladeshis live in villages and agriculture is their main (but meagre) source of income. The extended access to electricity that photovoltaic technology brings has improved the rural economy by creating new jobs as extended hours of light allow people to set up and run small businesses. Increasing numbers of people are employed to teach about and implement photovoltaic technology. The Solar Home System frees households from dependence on imported fuels like kerosene and diesel. Replacing kerosene improves the quality of people's lives: kitchens are safer and less smoky. Women and men are saved walking long distances to fetch kerosene - freeing precious time for income generating activities.

Mujibur Rahman, *General Manager, Grameen Shakti:* A major obstacle for many households remains repayment of the loans over the currently stipulated three year period. A monthly repayment starts at three hundred taka a month (about five dollars) and rises to eight or nine hundred taka, depending on what system you have. That is too much for the many millions of extremely poor households in Bangladesh. The Clean Development Mechanism revenue is unfortunately very small against the capital cost. But the people who are our clients are so poor that even that tiny amount of money would help them afford a Solar Home System. It could extend the payment period from three to say five years. And that would make all the difference to them, to their children.

PROJECT BENEFICIARIES

Abdul Rahim: I am a university student at home for the summer. We did not have electricity before these panels. So before, after dark we couldn't study. We used kerosene lamps but we couldn't see properly. Now we can work till really late at night. It works quite well and it is reliable. When I came home before I felt bad because there was no electricity. But now I like it. My father will buy a TV later. For now we are running a mobile phone. I couldn't survive now if they took the electricity away.

Alim Uz Zaman: I have my own phone business. To call from here to Dhaka is five taka. You can call internationally. From here to UK for a minute is 60 taka. It's a good price. You can phone Saudi Arabia, America, UK, anywhere. I have a minimum fifteen, twenty up to one hundred calls. Yesterday I had a very good day – good calls. The electricity comes from the Grameen solar panels. I could not run my business without electricity. I pay my bill to the bank every month. I also make a profit. Minimum five, eight, nine thousand a month above expenses. I put it in the bank or use it for my other business.

Before I had the phone – I went to Saudi Arabia to work for sixteen years. I missed Bangladesh. I came back because I could not have a wife or family – you cannot take your family there. My wife is a teacher – she teaches in high school here in the village. I earn enough now. I earned more in Saudi Arabia but now I have satisfaction and I have my family, my wife.

Hakim Uddin: With this electricity I keep my shop open till late. I do better business now.

Abdul Rahim and his family now benefit from the solar home system.

56

ELECTRIC VEHICLES FOR PUBLIC TRANSPORT

Projected savings: 11 000 – 14 000 tons of carbon dioxide annually

The introduction of three thousand new electric vehicles in Dhaka City is planned to add to the city's passenger transport system and to reduce local pollution.

Dhaka, the capital of Bangladesh and the largest city, has ten million residents who use rickshaws, cars, buses, motorbikes and taxis to get around. There are some private cars but most city dwellers and outside commuters depend on the public transport system. These electric vehicles will help to provide pollution free passenger services. The estimated lifetime of these electric vehicles is about ten years and they will operate on five routes in the city. Charging stations will be set up to recharge the batteries with grid electricity. The project owner is Rahim Afrooz, a private company. Beneficiaries are Dhaka's citizens (they will get cleaner air) and the vehicle owners and drivers who will have an improved (and blissfully silent) working environment. It will save between eleven and fourteen thousand tons of carbon dioxide over ten years.

Except the horns are so loud that they could give you a heart attack.

Atiq Rahman: Rahim Afrooz, the project owner, is an enlightened private company and we have a long standing relationship. We are using our social capital of relationships, a value that cannot be quantified easily. The enormous value of the social capital, of social relationships that we have formed over the years, we are bringing into the Clean Development Mechanism arena.

Babu: The electric vehicle project is not that big, but in terms of the management it is not easy because it is has many different stakeholders. We have the drivers' association, an owners' association, we have a vehicle supplier, and we have a battery supplier, a charging station. But we like difficulties. The Clean Development Mechanism projects can contribute to sustainable development and we want to see something tangible.

Khandakar Mainuddin: Bangladesh's environmental problems have changed. They used to be mainly deforestation and loss of biodiversity. Now it is industrial pollution, water pollution and air pollution because of urbanisation and industrialisation.

Moinul Islam Sharif: Rahim Afrooz had a long term plan to use electric vehicles because they had seen it done in Kathmandu. I went to Nepal and I found the electric vehicles fascinating - so clean and quiet. Except the horns are so loud that they could give you a heart attack – they have to be like that because the vehicles are so quiet. I had to get a friend who also knows the owner of Rahim Afrooz to convince him to see me. I went to see him and he said to me 'If I reduce carbon dioxide then northern countries will give me dollars?'

'Yes,' I said.

'How?' So I explained the Clean Development Mechanism and the Kyoto protocol.

'No, no, no,' he said. 'This is going all above my head. Give it to me very simply: one two three four five points. Write down five bullet points and give it to me.'

So we did and we went through the five points one by one. He asked will I be making money from selling hot air? And we said yes. How much money will I get out of this? And we explained that it depended on how we structure the project design and the business plan. He said do I have to spend any money? And we said no. So he said 'Go ahead. Do it. I don't mind.'

PROJECT PARTICIPANT

So we worked it out. I told him we need letters of authorisation from them, a signed memorandum of understanding, and that sometimes they would have to come to meetings. So he said DONE! We had to run after them even a year back. Now they call us up and say 'What happened? We want to do it.' We calculated the price on current values. The carbon price is ridiculously low: there is almost no money in it. And we asked him 'Are you still interested in it?' And he said 'Yes, absolutely.'

The business plan is based on subsidised charging stations for replacement of the batteries. There are recharging stations for the batteries so that the vehicles can go back after six or seven hours of carrying people. The charging time is about eight hours. They won't drive at night so this will help with charging. They will drive in specific routes – short routes. The weather is not conducive to walking in Bangladesh - it is either hot or raining.

Munawar Misbah Moin, *Chief Operating Officer, Rahim Afrooz:*
This is an environmentally friendly vehicle but there are some political problems. There is a lobby promoting big buses – but for those you need a lot of money. These vehicles are about twenty thousand dollars. If this project proves to be feasible then we can start on large projects and work on reducing the price.

59

IJAZ HOSSEIN
The Helio Monitor, Bangladesh

The two projects that Bangladesh has chosen are really good from the sustainable development point of view. In terms of carbon trading these are fairly small projects and are very limited. They are not very good projects from a purely commercial, business point of view, project which will be easily achievable. But if you are looking for projects which have very, very strong sustainable development angles, then you cannot choose easy projects.

If these projects by non-profit environmental organisations don't go through, it will be a real shame, because the Clean Development Mechanism will then just become a way to get credits by dumping a little bit of cash here and there. There will be paperwork, and maybe government intentions will be genuine, but sustainable development, which is supposed to be achieved along with the carbon emission reduction, will hardly be achieved. If the kinds of projects that we are developing are not given some kind of priority in the Clean Development Mechanism, if they do not have some kind of a niche there, a reserved area in the Clean Development Mechanism community, then these efforts will be wiped out.

Many expert consultants in developing countries are getting involved, but these people have absolutely no interest in sustainable development, absolutely no commitment to it, yet they get involved. Why? Because there's money, and all they have to do is play the game correctly, show some minor sustainable development benefits, and these projects will probably get through.

But local environmental organisations are in an excellent position to be able to deliver, to do the kind of work needed to bring integrity to the clean development mechanism. But these people are going to lose out if the global community which is promoting the Kyoto Protocol and Clean Development Mechanism does not protect them as it should.

SouthSouthNorth is an excellent project because of the capacity it's building in developing countries. Bangladesh is a poor country. This is almost a luxury. This kind of work can only be done because of funding and so the local environmental work, the sustainable development angle of the Clean Development Mechanism, can be emphasized.

SouthSouthNorth has been enormously beneficial in terms of the capacity that has been built through these projects. It is very definitely raising levels of expertise and capability. Certainly in Bangladesh people did not have very much experience before with developing Clean Development Mechanism projects.

Ijaz Hossain is associate professor, department of chemical engineering at Bangladesh University of Engineering and Technology. He has over fifteen years of experience in the field of chemical engineering with an emphasis on energy and the environment both as a teacher/researcher and as a consultant engineer. Since 1990, he has been involved in climate change activities, pertaining especially to energy related matters. In 1992, in collaboration with TERI, he completed a preliminary Greenhouse Gas emission calculation and costing for mitigation options for Bangladesh. Since then, he has been involved in several projects related to mitigation of greenhouse gases, most important of which is the Asia Least-Cost Greenhouse Gas Abatement Strategy project, where, he worked both as a national technical expert and as an international technical expert. As an international technical expert, he undertook technical missions to Mongolia and Myanmar

INDONESIA
accounting for the environment

A lot of problems, economic problems, development problems, environmental problems, are really social problems. If you address the social part of the problem you take care of the environmental part of the problem.

Agus Sari, *Team Leader, SouthSouthNorth*

INDONESIA is strung across the equator, an exquisite necklace of islands that embraces a myriad cultures and languages and startling biodiversity. Indonesia, like other developing countries, is an agricultural nation that depends on its ample natural resources. This makes it vulnerable to extreme weather, climate change and rising sea levels. Indonesia, a middle income country, is the fourth most populous in the world. Its sprawling cities consume more and more resources as Indonesia industrialises and demands increasing amounts of energy. There are hard choices that need to be made about Indonesia's development path.

Beneath its luxurious (and pillaged) forests and fertile farmlands are rich seams of natural gas, oil and coal. Indonesia has many energy choices: oil, natural gas and coal, but these are fossil fuels and sooner or later they will be used up.

At the current rate of use oil will be out of the scenario by 2020 and perhaps natural gas by 2030 or 2040. There is a lot of coal but it is of low quality. So the only choice would be to use abundantly available resources: solar energy, geothermal, wind, and small hydro projects as this nation is very mountainous. There is a great deal of agricultural waste that can be converted into power very easily with current technology. If these resources are utilised then the use of fossil fuels can be slowed down, especially oil, which is also an export commodity. The use of renewable energy is environmentally benign and will improve the quality of the air.

Concern for climate change is shared between the South and the North. Indonesia's priority is ensuring continued economic and social development. However, increased development leads to higher energy consumption, resulting in higher greenhouse gas emissions. SouthSouthNorth in Indonesia has taken on complex Clean Development Mechanism projects that seek equity and development for the South while contributing to the protection of the global climate through piloting renewable energy and agricultural projects. A particularly challenging project is in the city of Yogyakarta, the cultural centre of Central Java. The aim is to provide cleaner, more efficient public transport to an increasingly choked city. While transport projects are especially complex, they are necessary for equitably accounting for the environment.

VOICES FROM INDONESIA

Armely Meiviana, *SouthSouthNorth:* Changes in the climate will affect my own future. Any island country will be greatly affected – particularly by a sea level rise. And the seasons – we did not have any seasons but lately we feel that things are changing – we had really bad floods last year in Jakarta. We cannot be really sure if it is climate change. But as I read more and more I become very concerned. Not many people know about climate change and very few people are aware that what they are doing now can have a really bad effect in the future.

Climate change is not a popular issue in Indonesia. So now I don't even use the words climate change – I talk about issues like air pollution, transportation, energy. Environmental protection in Indonesia is very poor. I see that young people consume avidly. Consumption has an impact on the environment. I worry about how to teach them effective consumption: that you buy what you need to buy, not just what you want. They need to learn that what they do – that everything they buy – will have an impact, positive or negative.

Olivia Tanujaya, *SouthSouthNorth:* I decided to focus on the environmental issues because it's something that people just don't care about in Indonesia. They are concerned about the economy and money. We have abundant natural resources, but if we don't manage them well they will be lost.

Danang Parikesit, *SouthSouthNorth:* If you want to market public transport, you must market it to the younger generation. They are the future owners of the whole world – if you show young children the good case of sustainable development you can make sure that the knowledge is in their blood and affects how they behave.

Setiyoso, *Head of Transport. Yogyakarta:* A perfect world is when all of the people come to a realisation about the environment. The first step is an individual's realisation, the second is law enforcement. If each individual understood why we need fresh air, plants, animals, if that's understood, it will be great. At this time law enforcement is not working everywhere, including on the buses. But if it worked, everything will be fine. It is about those two things: knowledge of the environment and law enforcement.

The 1ˢᵗ step is an individual's realisation, the 2ⁿᵈ is law enforcement. If each individual understood why we need fresh air, plants, animals, if that's understood, it will be great.

AGUS SARI
Team Leader, SouthSouthNorth, Indonesia

The level of rigour and the hands on involvement that SouthSouthNorth has is unique.

Certainly we have not had it before. The skill sharing, the rigour of project planning, the screening, the methodological way of looking at things, has been beneficial. It has forced us to be really up to speed with the latest methods of accounting for emissions, with appraising sustainability, that puts us right on a par with institutions in the North. I have learned a lot. Personally the value of this for my own personal development is that I value that kind of friendship, that kind of social network. The SouthSouthNorth projects in Indonesia have been complicated – deliberately so. The biggest motivation was to go into things where we would learn. The link between local issues and the global rule making process, the capacity building – this is so complicated. We add to this a complicated process. We underestimated it – the Clean Development Mechanism is complicated in the first place. But the good part is that we all learned a great deal.

The longer term solution to the climate problem is decarbonisation. The largest factor, the one that is the time bomb, is transportation. Transportation is complicated by nature because it is especially broad and it involves a huge number of stakeholders. There is no such thing as a transport sector, or policy – it is manufacturing and road building, traffic, government. It is a labyrinth.

Because of the complications it needs to be dealt with properly, but no one knows how to deal with transportation properly. The fuel used in transport is already the largest in Indonesia's energy sector. We need to do something and we are using the Clean Development Mechanism to deal with the problems with energy use in the transportation sector. There is a lot of work for a very small global benefit. We are making buses greener – and it makes the local air quality better. The global reduction is small but we are tackling this problem in an integrated way by exploring how to implement a better transport system.

Agus Sari is Executive Director of Pelangi. He has an advanced degree from the University of California at Berkeley. He also serves as an Advisor to the Indonesian Delegation to Climate Negotiations and is currently in charge of developing the national authority for the clean development mechanism approval process on behalf of the Ministry of Environment in Indonesia.

MOEKTI SOEJACHMOEN
SouthSouthNorth

I love working with SouthSouthNorth. I really must say it is the best group I ever had, talking about the international group.

I really like this whole SouthSouthNorth process. It is great dealing with different people, with different opinions on the Clean Development Mechanism. Also sharing what we work on with the rest of the SouthSouthNorth group. They are just so helpful to each other and I just don't want to miss this group. That is why when they were talking about a future phase during one of our meetings, I was like 'We have to do this, we have to work together.'

I think that this good feeling helps get the work done. We had an evaluation here in 2000 in Jakarta. It was hard for everyone because we had to submit a list of our potential projects, go through the list and choose two from each country. It was difficult – we have not reached the same level in the four countries – but the atmosphere helped us all interact constructively with each other. It is not easy here in Indonesia to push the government to do something on the Clean Development Mechanism as they also have other priorities. We have some issues we still have to work on – each country has its own issues at national level – but it is has worked well.

EMISSION REDUCTIONS
FOR URBAN BUSES

Projected savings: 9 600 tons of carbon dioxide over seven years

This project is designed to improve the public transport system in Yogyakarta by using cleaner engines in two hundred out of the five hundred buses in the area, restructuring urban public transport management, improving routing and schedules, as well as through introducing alternative fuels.

The project participants are the Yogyakarta Urban Public Transport Alliance. This alliance is made up of three participants: the Center of Transportation and Logistics Studies, Gadjah Mada University, which will manage the project and deal with related technical issues, and the Yogyakarta Urban Bus Cooperative, the owner and operator of the buses in the area. The Road Traffic and Transport Office of the local government of Yogyakarta issues the licences for public buses. The beneficiaries are the project participants and Yogya residents – the passengers on the public buses and those who live around the routes. Total emission reduction for the seven year crediting period of the project is about nine thousand six hundred tons of carbon dioxide.

Danang Parikesit, *SouthSouthNorth Facilitator, Yogyakarta:* Our research looks at the link between transport and sustainable development. Public transport is so bad in Yogya that patronage is going down. The reason that we are losing our patronage is because it is not promoted. It is not very safe, it is not secure. The buses have very bad engines that are not maintained properly – so the city is polluted. There are several options available to do the emission reductions. We came to the choice of replacing the current diesel engines with liquid petroleum gas engines. But this needs to be refined and discussed with the bus owners, who will have to pay for the change. This will be the major challenge. How to deal with this sort of technology change? Two hundred buses and eighty owners – it is a headache, a challenge.

72

The value of the Yogya project does not lie in the amount of emission reductions for sale. The value of our project is that it is the first transport project in the Clean Development Mechanism. The emission reduction of this project is quite marginal but its future value will have an impact on a much larger scale. It is important that the private sector is participating in development, and that is a very new thing. That is what is so valuable about our approach.

Look at the heart of the matter of the Clean Development Mechanism: it is giving people in government and the private sector the opportunity to reduce global emissions. It really is these two things – it puts developing countries at a similar level in the global effort to reduce emissions. But it also gives the opportunity to access the world's financial resources, to lift up the barriers that are currently experienced by many public transport operators in Indonesia. I see the potential as very large, very big. We are very proud of our transport project as it is the first of its kind.

We have a unique approach in this SouthSouthNorth project: We are encouraging a coalition to be built between the local government, bus co-operatives and our centres. We have to communicate the ideas – this is more important now than the technical aspects. They have regular meetings – kind of social gatherings – it is good that they have the sort of forums where we can put forward the Clean Development Mechanism using simple terms and explanations. SouthSouthNorth has been an eye opener to opportunities. It has prompted us to look with a different perspective on how we define development.

One of the main problems for improving the transport system is finance. So it fits together really with the idea of the Clean Development Mechanism. One way we should be more pro-active is with investors – to show that it really works, that investors can be found. This would really help us convince people. It has not been done before and we don't have any evidence. If it works we will be the cutting edge so we take it as a challenge but we need some support. The really tricky part is to get someone to buy the emissions reduced. We have not gone through this in any other projects. That is why the role of SouthSouthNorth is very important – so that once the emission reduction is verified we can bring it to transaction. Meaning that we can demonstrate what we told people earlier.

Theoretically the owners and the drivers are convinced. But you only really believe once you have the money in your hand after the transaction and you can buy new vehicles.

73

PROJECT PARTICIPANT

Setiyoso, *Head of the Yogyakarta Region Transport:* The problem with the city's public transport is not just the pollution it causes but also the quality of the transport system itself. I would say emissions are the biggest problem. There are many complaints from the public especially about the smoke, the thick smoke. Many people use masks, especially people using motorcycles, to avoid the smog. If the proposal succeeds and we can sell carbon, that will subsidise the co-operative to work more efficiently. We want to enforce regulations, but the owners hesitate to change. As long as the income of the bus driver and the bus owner decreases, it will be difficult. With extra money, hopefully it will be able to function. This is just a starting point. This is one learning process about the Clean Development Mechanism. As someone who understands the environment, I think carbon trading can help the developing countries. In the developed countries it will be much harder to reduce emissions, because they are already efficient. The industry is already efficient, the cars are already good, and it is hard to decrease it. So this is a good opportunity for the developing countries, it can be used as capital as we can quite easily reduce our carbon emissions.

Vita, *Centre for Transportation and Logistics Studies, University of Gajah Mada:* Maybe the final goal of the Clean Development Mechanism, apart from emission reductions, is to improve the management of the co-operative and of the operator. Replacement of the buses is required. So, the Clean Development Mechanism would help the bus owners manage the reduction of emissions.

Olivia Tanujaya, *SouthSouthNorth:* I have had such an interesting experience with this project. We conducted training for all the team members. Most of them didn't know about the Clean Development Mechanism, it was a whole new concept. What is interesting is that they got really interested, particularly in working as a group. That made me see how this process is good for people.

PROJECT BENEFICIARIES

My name is Kirmanto. *I am an owner of a Yogyakarta Kopata Bus:* With the Clean Development Mechanism project there will be many advantages. Clearly there will more passengers. Better buses will make it easier to get passengers and to improve the bus's income. With a new bus, damages rarely happen. Therefore there is a guarantee in the operational flow and the operational cost is lower because they are in good condition. The obstacle is that if it is on credit, the return is temporarily imbalanced or uneven.

My name is Inung. *I am a bus passenger.* I walk from my house and then I wait for the bus under a tree. It takes me thirty minutes to get to work. The bus is not that big, it's dirty. Sometimes the chairs are broken. People get on and off the bus wherever they like. The drivers speed and stop and wait for the passengers everywhere. There are no bus stops. I would like more safety from the pickpockets. Sometimes we cannot open the windows at all, so it's hot inside because there is no air-conditioning. We do not know when the buses are going to

There are many complaints from the public especially about the smoke, the thick smoke. Many people use masks to avoid the smog.

I am Bambang Priatno. *I am the driver of bus number 162. Yogyakarta Kopata Bus:* Why did I become a driver? I didn't complete school, so I worked with my father as a mechanic. I turned to driving when my father passed away. And for the daily operational problems, I also feel the happiness and sadness as a Kopata's driver. The daily average income is very low for the driver now. We were bound to pay a daily rental fee. We cannot fulfil the targets because people don't travel on the buses. The drivers and co-operative are considered as work partners. So we do not differentiate a driver and an employer. We need each other. The driver needs an employer; the employer/owner needs a driver. Our daily rental fee is based on *tepo seliro*. That is a Javanese term for sharing and toleration. So it is not only us who suffer if we cannot fulfil the target.

come. We would like to have a regular schedule of the bus. I am willing to pay a little more for the buses to be in better condition than they are now. I prefer the bus, because we don't have to think about the street. I just sit down on the bus. It is more relaxing and it decreases the traffic as well. There are more people in one vehicle as well. It is environmentally friendly. It means that there are less private cars, ojek, motorcycles or even taxi. The air will be better.

75

THE BANDARJAYA **RICE HUSK POWER PLANT** PROJECT

The Bandarjaya Rice Husk Power Plant Project, a small scale power plant project located in the village of Bandarjaya in Sumatra, is expected to generate three megawatts of electricity. There will be ten small rice mills involved in this project, annually producing sixty thousand tons of rice husks in a twenty square kilometre area. The plant can potentially supply electricity to about eight thousand five hundred households. The project participants are PT Lunto Bioenergi Prima, the local bio-energy company, and Bronzeoak, a United Kingdom based specialist in renewable energy. The local beneficiaries are rice mill owners, the state electricity company, PLN; local electricity consumers; the local construction industry and local manufacturers of power plant equipment. Emission reduction willl be fourteen thousand tons carbon dioxide a year over ten years

THE COMBINED **SOLAR, WIND AND BIOMASS** PROCESSING UNIT

The Combined Solar, Wind and Biomass for Small Agricultural Processing Unit integrates renewable energy sources to operate a small agricultural processing unit in the drying of food. This processing unit will in turn increase the added value of agriculture and marine products and simultaneously initiate the industrialisation process in the rural areas.

The drying machine, designed by and patented by the Centre for Research on Engineering Application in Tropical Agriculture at the Bogor Agriculture Institute, will improve the quality of food products and minimise the risk of failure due to unpredictable weather. It is also expected to benefit the local farmers and fishermen by increasing their incomes. The solar dryer equipments will be distributed to the local cooperatives under six percent per annum micro-credit system with less than three years to repay. The project participant is Bogor Agricultural Institute. The beneficiaries are local farmers and fishermen, local cooperatives and the local authority. Emission reduction will be nine thousand tons carbon dioxide each year for ten years.

LOLO PANGGABEAN AND NINA NATALINA
The Helio Monitors, Indonesia

The Clean Development Mechanism projects have a very heavy emphasis on public participation in the approval of the project. People must approve it, local government must approve it – all the stakeholders must approve it. One of the requirements of Clean Development Mechanism projects is that they are sustainable in every sense: economically, socially and environmentally.

In the Yogya transport project we worked together and discussed how to monitor from the beginning. Everyone sat there and thought about the project design, about how to make the project work. SouthSouthNorth included all the stakeholders in the team. Everyone works together on how to make the project work – the bus drivers, the organisers of the bus drivers, local government and fuel suppliers, so there is discussion at all times and at all levels. Objections from people on the street are not very likely as what is proposed is a better and cleaner bus system.

The bus project is a very good and clean and astute project. But from the point of view of emission reductions it is very small. I don't know who will be interested in it. But it is a very good development project.

Lolo Marangkup Panggabean received his doctorate in Nuclear Physics (Experimental) at Michigan State University in 1972. He has done developmental work in the field of renewable energy for the last twenty two years, and works closely with the government and utilities for energy policy placement and energy planning. For the last six years, he has been the Renewable Energy Co-ordinator with Yayasan Bina Usaha Lingkungan promoting renewable energy as a means of environmental protection.

Nina Natalina, the programme manager at Yayasan Bina Usaha Lingkungan, has extensive experience in community based environmental conservation activities related to biodiversity and renewable energy. She obtained her M.B.A. in General Management from Institute Pengembangan Manajemen Indonesia, Jakarta.

SOUTH AFRICA
accounting for people

We have low levels of consumption in the developing world. You can either suppress demand and keep people poor, or you can develop. That means allowing people to consume energy and satisfy their service demands. We have got to go there: we can't take the path of saying let's keep people poor in order to reduce emissions. But we can do a lot to influence the direction of their consumption so as to avoid emissions before they happen.

Steve Thorne, *Team Leader SouthSouthNorth, South Africa*

SOUTH AFRICA, at the confluence of the Indian and the Atlantic Oceans, is the economic engine of southern Africa. Despite being energy and mineral rich, South Africa grapples to reach across the income and energy rift dividing her citizens. This is the bitter legacy of three centuries of colonialism and apartheid, a system that deliberately enriched a minority by the suppression and enforced impoverishment of the majority. Attaining social equity has been central to South Africa's development ideals since the realisation of democracy in 1994. The expansion of affordable energy services to all its citizens is crucial if years of legislated inequity are to be redressed.

South Africa is, however, the biggest emitter of greenhouse gases in Africa, producing half of Africa's emissions. It has a highly developed economy that flourishes within the context of great unemployment and extreme poverty.

So, while taking care of South Africa's development trajectory, the vulnerability of its poor as well as environmental degradation and pollution need special attention. It is essential that South Africa's energy-hungry industry and mining sectors, attracted by low cost energy in the form of coal and electricity, buy into the costly task of emission reduction. This is a distinct possibility as the implications of the Clean Development Mechanism are explored at project and policy level. There is great potential for sustainable local development projects that afford the global benefit of reducing greenhouse gases.

The South African team has chosen projects that display a wide spectrum of Clean Development Mechanism potentialities. One project fits low cost houses with ceilings and ceiling insulation, energy efficient lamps and solar water heaters, leapfrogging a community from suppressed energy consumption into clean technology. Another project, with a large corporate paper manufacturer, is exploring ways of reducing emissions through increasing the proportion of renewable energy in the paper industry, extending the life of the plant and the jobs it provides. A third project explores ways of tapping methane from a city landfill to provide cleaner-burning fuel for local industries. This could channel money for poverty alleviation into the adjacent residential area. It will also generate income for a cash strapped city whose obligation to manage its waste sometimes competes with poverty alleviation strategies. These projects actually extend the ways in which the Clean Development Mechanism can be made to account for social equity by improving the quality of people's lives.

VOICES FROM SOUTH AFRICA

Elsie Tabalaza, *Kuyasa resident:* Things are much better. Since the ceilings have been installed in my house it is much warmer and more beautiful than it was before.

Shirene Rosenberg, *SouthSouthNorth:* I tell anyone who cares to listen about climate change and energy efficiency. For most people it's a fascinating topic which they've always considered to be far removed from their daily lives. If you explain suddenly people start realising that it affects their lives directly.

I want to see these wondrous things, which many of us see as everyday, moving into poor people's lives.

Steve Thorne, *Team Leader. SouthSouthNorth:* I want to see these wondrous things, which many of us see as everyday, moving into poor people's lives. I am excited that at lower cost people can still get the level of energy service they want. And they can get it now, as opposed to in the future.

Lwandle Mqadi, *SouthSouthNorth:* The Clean Development Mechanism needs time, it needs a change in mindset not only from people from the South but from people who are supposed to come here and buy the emissions. After all it's a market. In the end this market is going to determine whether people want to invest and what kind of investment Southern countries will get. It is not about people coming and getting their oil and then leaving.

Jeff Jenet, *Financial Consultant:* Corporates want to extract every last cent. Here you have projects that can both make money in and of themselves and that improve the environment.

84

STEVE THORNE
Team Leader, SouthSouthNorth, South Africa

How do you enthral a community of project developers? The way you do that is by showing that this is going to work across the board.

I am hooked into the area of climate change that is about cleaning up the energy service of South Africa. It links into my life, my children's lives, right into the future. It changes the way people think about how to do things. My personal interest is not so much climate change for itself, but in seeing how a flexible instrument like the Clean Development Mechanism can drive the energy economy from business as usual to a cleaner kind of development. This possibility has opened up because of individuals who have been looking at ways of reducing energy costs, looking at the externalities – the costs that are currently not included in the price. The Clean Development Mechanism credits one of those externalities and gives it real force. In other words by using energy services that are less polluting, you get credits against what would have happened otherwise. That is a bit of beauty.

We chose the South African projects to achieve a spread. We have tried to stretch it from the most inappropriate to the most energy consumptive sectors. How do you enthral a community of potential project investors? You do this by showing that this is going to work across the board. That it will work in situations where there is abject poverty, such as in low cost housing. That it will work in industrial situations where it is all about profit margins. We develop a huge sense of humour just playing with ideas and how they develop, contrasting what would have happened with what we are planning. It has to do with changing trajectories of development. I like the idea that the money we can raise through the Clean Development Mechanism can go into poverty alleviation. The possibilities are huge with such a mundane thing as a dump. That is weird and it is lovely. These are little miracles.

With the industrial projects it is about shifting priorities on projects where there are huge emission reductions. It is a matter of tweaking them from second best projects to the very best projects within the constraints of what the company has to spend. The possibilities are hugely increased and enhanced by the potential for carbon trading: things move right up the agenda.

We need to think down the track to understand the global implications. There are so many countries that develop policy that is not led by primary research, not even by secondary research. Our research is proving to be of real value here. Suddenly we are on the brink of understanding what the real costs will be, what the real implications to the treasury are for shifts in the energy sector, that you can put money into more deserving areas. Our projects are helping us to understand how we can use the little bit of treasury leverage we have in our country to drive policy with real implications for people.

I have loved dealing with a team of people who have gone from no knowledge to exceptional knowledge. They are now people who are leaders in their field, having wrestled with Clean Development Mechanism projects, understanding what the implications are of doing the project-led approach to policy development. That is key to what we are about.

Steve Thorne is an energy engineer
who has worked in the fields of energy
policy formulation and advocacy, and
project design over the past 15 years.
His work has aimed at transforming
the energy economy towards more
sustainable energy supply and use. Over
the past 10 years he has worked at the
Energy and Development Research
Centre on policy options for adequate
and affordable energy services for the
rural poor focussing on energy efficiency
and run his own consultancy known as
Energy Transformations CC. He is technical
co-ordinator of the SouthSouthNorth
project and leads the South Africa
SouthSouthNorth team. Amongst other
recent work, Steve has designed and
evaluated projects as lead international
consultant for the Global Environment
Facility in South Africa, Namibia, Malawi
and Uganda. Steve also serves as an expert
panellist on small scale projects under
the Clean Development Mechanism's
Executive Board and is currently writing
a doctoral thesis on the transfer and
receptivity of clean energy technology
through the climate window

87

Why bother about environmental issues when people's livelihoods are at stake and people are struggling to just stay alive?

SHIRENE ROSENBERG
Project Manager, SouthSouthNorth

LWANDLE MQADI
Technical Team Member, SouthSouthNorth

Initially what interested me was that this would be something where I would feel that I would be able to make a difference, in terms of contributing towards people's quality of life locally. I remember thinking that this would be one of those things where you would be able to sleep with a clear conscience. You do realise that not everything is as idyllic as it appears, but this group is working towards real change.

Initially it was difficult for me. Why bother about environmental issues when people's livelihoods are at stake and people are struggling to just stay alive? Then you start realising that the two are not separated, that it is linked to natural disasters, the diversion of government expenditure to places where it would otherwise not have gone. These things are affected by climate change, which has an impact on people's social and economic well-being.

The South-South links are very interesting. There has been a switch from being a recipient to being an initiator. I was fortunate because two weeks after I started with SouthSouthNorth we went to a United Nations conference in New Delhi, and it was amazing. In two weeks I had to absorb everything and you get bombarded with all of these issues from every angle. The whole SouthSouthNorth crowd was there, we were all staying in the same hotel and so it was a good bonding experience. I feel there's a sense of family. On a global level people had respect for the work we were doing. I was sitting there thinking this is like poetry. I was really proud to be associated with SouthSouthNorth. I think they get it right because they're honest, there's a bond and there's a common commitment.

We are not an operating agency ourselves; we facilitate projects so we find that a lot of people come with different experiences from different sectors. This is not just about the work, it's also about the people you work with. It all depends on interaction with people because the better the interaction the more information you can get from them. We work with industry and with the public sector. I think it is amazing that one concept can actually be applied to so many different sectors. Each and every sector of the country is involved.

I am involved in technical issues. Everybody is still learning: there are only a few people in the whole world who know about the Clean Development Mechanism. It's a new thing but it appeals to me. The methodology, the way people think about a problem, the analysis behind the project design, the fact that you put numbers and figures next to everything, developing it into a process, a tool that works and that can be emulated.

ENERGY EFFICIENT **HOUSING** IN KUYASA

Projected savings: 5500 tons of carbon dioxide avoided annually

We are setting a precedent internationally for developing this multi-lateral convention as a way to directly address poverty alleviation.

This project activity intervenes in an existing low income housing development project in Kuyasa, Khayelitsha. This is a pilot of ten houses and the plan is to upgrade many more houses in the future. The project owner is the City of Cape Town and the beneficiaries are the participating households in Kuyasa. The project activity improves the thermal performance of the housing units through the introduction of ceilings, energy efficient lighting and solar water heaters. This reduces electricity and kerosene consumption per household, reduces carbon emissions and reduces air pollution with subsequent decreases in pulmonary pneumonia, carbon monoxide poisoning and other respiratory illnesses. A decrease in accidents such as the ingestion of kerosene and burns and damage to property as a result of fire is also anticipated. Improved end-use efficiency combined with the use of solar energy for water heating will result in measurable energy consumption savings. This contributes to 'energy poverty' alleviation and will save five thousand five hundred tons of carbon dioxide annually.

Steve Thorne, *SouthSouthNorth:* If people are poor or lack access to energy infrastructure such as fuels and appliances, they are 'energy poor'. But if development means anything it surely means increasing livelihoods and with this the ability to consume goods and services. That includes energy services. This implies that currently amongst the poor there is 'suppressed demand' for energy services. Without interventions, this group would acquire the technologies, the fuels and the behaviour that has resulted in the need for emissions targets in the first place. We can reverse future problems by intervening now.

The key thing is how to deal with avoiding emissions that would otherwise have happened in the future. I have seen in my past work in energy efficiency and the provision of affordable energy services to the urban and rural poor, that the poor are amazingly adept at managing their energy services within the constraints of what they have access to. It is worth building on that management ability to take it to the next stage and enable people to leapfrog to new technologies so they can continue that same level of management with better tools to do it. If we can make a major intervention in Kuyasa we can set a precedent for making a major intervention internationally by using the climate convention to address poverty alleviation directly.

Lwandle Mqadi: After the pilot of ten houses a rollout of more than two thousand houses is expected based on SouthSouthNorth's findings. And there are another million houses to go. You've got to think in the future, make a projection. We argue that these people, as their income increases, as the development strategy of the City is implemented, will use more electricity. We have to find ways of avoiding those emissions. We have also done a lot of anthropological surveys to see how people use these new technologies, how they feel about them and how they affect their disposable income. If the argument for suppressed demand succeeds the future of development will look very different and be much more efficient.

PROJECT PARTICIPANT

Osman Asmal, *Environmental Co-ordinator, City of Cape Town:* We considered one of the difficulties of the Clean Development Mechanism with the Kuysasa Project: How to make it real on the ground, and how to explain what climate change is all about. Kuyasa was an easy project with which to demonstrate this to city councillors and the community. We can use it to show what the Clean Development Mechanism is, how it can deal with social issues, and improve people's quality of life. The benefits are clear. The physical interventions in the houses have already been demonstrated with solar heating for hot water and the ceilings have made the houses significantly warmer. The one thing that stands out for me on a more personal level is listening to people talk about how these ceilings affect their lives. It gives the house more warmth than just a standard low cost house. People talk about these things and how they improve their lives. We can take people from the community and from outside and show what the benefits are.

..ceilings, energy efficient lighting and solar water heaters.

SouthSouthNorth came up with great technical information. The City brings the community to the table and plays a facilitating role. We have championed this project. It is crucial to get senior political buy in. It has been a very good capacity building experience for the city, for SouthSouthNorth and for the community workers. We have been testing, seeing what works and what doesn't. It is a good example of how you can get things done with different role players. It shows that if different partners put their minds to a problem you can come up with new and effective solutions. You can play to each other's strengths.

PROJECT BENEFICIARIES

Rendani Kharivhe, *Agama Energy. SouthSouthNorth Technical Supervisors:* SouthSouthNorth contracted us to handle the technical side. This was a demonstration project to show people the technology. Many had heard about renewable energy, but they needed a concrete example. SouthSouthNorth needed to do a baseline study so they wanted to monitor the performance of the houses and the technology.

This project has really showcased renewable energy technologies and sources. We have had a huge response from people in the area, as well as from people outside. I had a call from a lady in Harare, Zimbabwe, who also wanted the same technology. She went to see them and wants to have them fitted in her home.

Elsie Tabalaza, Things are much better. Since the ceilings have been installed, it is much warmer, and more beautiful than it was before. The solar water heater is also making a big difference. I don't have to put water on the flame or use the electric kettle. Many people have come to see, and they can't wait for the big project to come so they can get these things. I did not even know of these things before, so I wouldn't have bought it. Also, I would not have been able to afford it. It is a great pleasure to be one of the beneficiaries of the project because it has made my life easier.

54424: Elsie Tabalaza

 # 54979: Nomalizo Bhebheza
'We sell vegetables from the house, and the boys also go door to door selling them. The vegetables don't always sell.'

 # 55747: Victor Makwaba, The ceiling makes it much better.

 # 56290: Violet Nandipha Sgebenga and Yamkela
4 am: Mother wakes up. She catches a train at 5 am starts work at 6 am in the city centre.
8 am: Kids go to school
7 pm: Nandipha returns home from work
10 pm: all asleep

 # 54516: Thembisa Kulana, Many children come here to the crèche.

96

TOWN SOMETIMES

Phuduse 14 Years

PAMELA HLATANA BORN 12

WE EAT FRUIT

Phumeza 19 years

Phamela ...years

MONDI **ENERGY EFFICIENCY** PROJECTS

Recovery of biomass waste for use as renewable energy. Projected savings: 703 690 tons of carbon dioxide a year

Recovery of chemicals and steam generation. Projected savings: 69 000 tons carbon dioxide a year for ten years

97

The Project owner is Mondi Ltd, an Anglo American Group company. They are considering two possible Clean Development Mechanism projects.

The first proposes to recover biomass waste for use as a renewable energy alternative to coal for generating steam at Mondi Kraft, Richard's Bay. This proposed project will recover the biomass waste, currently being dumped in a landfill, to use as a renewable energy resource in biomass boilers. This will reduce coal consumption and other carbon dioxide emissions. The biomass boiler could accommodate a further one hundred and seventy tons per day which the coal boiler currently being used cannot carry. Reduction of carbon dioxide emissions is estimated at nearly seven hundred and four thousand tons annually over a crediting period of ten years from reduced coal burning and avoided methane emissions from land-filled biomass.

The second project proposes to recover chemicals and generate energy (steam) through the oxidation of organic components in the black liquor and recovery of chemicals at the Mondi Felixton Mill in Richards Bay. The Felixton Mill is located near Richards Bay, a harbour and industrial town. The mill uses bagasse, a waste product from sugarcane processing, to produce a corrugated medium paper material used in the manufacturing of packaging material.

The Felixton plant emits approximately five hundred and fifty four tons of carbon dioxide each day. The black liquor from cooking the bagasse is discharged into the sea, untreated. The project proposes to recover the black liquor and oxidise the organics to generate energy and release the inorganic component of the liquor (sodium) for re-use. The total carbon dioxide emissions reduced are calculated to be just below sixty nine thousand tons a year for the ten year crediting period.

Steve Thorne, *SouthSouthNorth:* The main idea is to entice corporate South Africa into starting to identify these kinds of projects for their own benefit as well as for the benefit of the people of South Africa. If we can show Mondi creating benefits for themselves with real projects that have been stringently checked out, it creates opportunities for other businesses that we know are very energy intensive: they have huge opportunities to increase efficiency. Mondi sees itself as a champion which is great. Corporates in South Africa looking to sell their products elsewhere in the world increasingly have to account for the environmental and social footprint that they leave behind in producing their products. It is interesting because it creates a possibility of getting project activities within the corporate sector that would not have happened otherwise. It has been fantastic to get in there and to see how the corporate world does things. The way in is through people with whom there is a resonance, an understanding of the possibilities of using the Clean Development Mechanism to push a project that would otherwise have been low down on their scale of priorities. I think we have been brutal about being stringent and accurate.

PROJECT PARTICIPANT: MONDI KRAFT

Ciska Terreblanche, *Mondi Kraft, Richards Bay:* I attended one of the Clean Development Mechanism workshops that Steve and Stefan at SouthSouthNorth presented. It appealed to me immediately because of the carbon trading potential. This gives the South credit when we do upgrade and reduce our carbon emissions. We have done beneficial projects but we got no financial recognition for it. It's good that for once there is an international, global goal that is driving everybody. Normally a company would be interested only in the local environment or community. Now, at last, you feel that you are part of a bigger scheme.

Because industry is such a dynamic world, project ideas are proposed and disapproved very rapidly. Industry weighs up whatever you put in front of them in terms of profit. The shareholders will not invest any money in a company if they know that the company takes unnecessary risks. So you need to demonstrate that your project has a good return. A project needs to be successful for others to see this. Industry is very averse to risk but you can work things out because there is money in the Clean Development Mechanism. It makes some marginal projects, good projects, financially viable and that will make them happen. The paper industry needs specialised

Corporates in South Africa looking to sell their products elsewhere in the world increasingly have to account for the environmental and social footprint that they leave behind in producing their products.

I talked Clean Development Mechanism so much, anywhere and anytime I had the opportunity I would talk about it, try to work it in. I think in the end that when people saw me coming they would think 'Oh, no, not Clean Development Mechanism again.' It is a matter of educating people slowly whenever you can. And people don't always want to understand it all. They just want to know 'What do I need to do to make it work?' Industry is like that. Especially the science guys. They are very sceptical about climate change, so you have to win them over.

equipment that we buy internationally. Yes, the money does shift from the South to the North. But by using the Clean Development Mechanism you can at least secure the future of a facility for another ten years of lifespan for that mill. You are then ensuring that the employees there will have work for another ten years. If we can do that then that is sustainable development.

SouthSouthNorth has benefited us. Because they have been part of the process, they have all the historic information and the contacts. They are trusted; they are credible, not only to us but also to international partners. SouthSouthNorth is a trusted entity from the investor's point of view. If they have gone through a project with you it becomes a lot more credible.

99

METHANE EXTRACTION FROM URBAN WASTE FOR INDUSTRIAL USE

Projected savings: 900 tons of carbon dioxide a year for project activity one

Projected savings: 1 246 to 1 277 tons carbon dioxide a year for project activity two

The project will recover and use landfill gas at Bellville South landfill site in Cape Town to generate renewable energy for subsequent use by the adjacent industrial community. The project owner is the City of Cape Town.

This project aims to transform an 'end of life' landfill into a 'renewable energy/waste recovery park', which is not only environmentally rehabilitated but also provides socio-economic spin offs for the adjacent industrial and residential communities by creating jobs (through onsite recycling units) and by providing renewable energy for a minimum of fifteen years. This will result in lower greenhouse gas emissions.

The proposed main project has two activities. **First:** the capture of gas that would otherwise have been emitted into the atmosphere. Emissions reduced will be nine hundred tons carbon dioxide per annum for this activity. **Second:** The use of the gas as a fuel that directly replaces fossil fuels used to generate steam and other energy services. This energy will be marketed for a minimum of fifteen years to selected adjacent industries. For the second project activity, the emissions avoided range between one thousand two hundred and forty six and one thousand two hundred and seventy seven tons of carbon dioxide a year.

Steve Thorne: The landfill projects are all about low hanging fruit because these kinds of projects are the cheapest way to reduce emissions. This is because of the methane which has a global warming effect more than twenty times greater than carbon dioxide. But there are ways of doing it that let you go beyond just flaring the gas and leaving it at that. We are looking at ways of enhancing sustainable development. We are exploring this in terms of institutional arrangements with the City of Cape Town and in setting up a community trust structure in addition to exploring the usefulness of the gas. The project is fortunately right next to an industrial estate and therefore has possibilities for marketing gas that most landfills will not have.

Tony Barbour, *SouthSouthNorth Project Facilitator:* This project is complex but part of what SouthSouthNorth does is to see what the institutional and technical requirements are, and to see where it can be streamlined to make it less expensive and less time consuming. Part of the challenge has been the steep learning curve for everyone.

Jeff Jennet, *Financial Analyst:* I knew a lot about projects but I did not know anything about landfill sites or the Clean Development Mechanism. It is an absolute eye-opener. It is so fascinating how you can use a landfill site and you can actually make it profitable. That just boggles the mind. Your comparison here is not the City of Cape Town taking ten rand and making eleven. In fact, where they were going to have to pay twenty rand, instead they will be making eleven. So you are protecting communities and you are saving government money. It is pulling in all the right directions. More money into government should find its way back into the community for further development. It is awesome.

PROJECT PARTICIPANT: CITY OF CAPE TOWN

Peter Novella, *Solid Waste Management:* We were very keen to get involved when we started to see how to use the methane from the landfill. We have to manage this anyway and it is a way to get some much needed cash into the city for the rehabilitation of the landfill. We can harness some income for projects like this which are viable because there is a need internationally for carbon credits.

The project looks viable. It is unique. We will be managing the landfill, reducing impact on the environment, reducing the amount of fossil fuel otherwise used, and thus reducing emissions. This project has developed capacity for senior level city council employees around the Clean Development Mechanism. There is the potential to do environmental good. That is important. We have to manage our gas pollution and the city can't otherwise afford to do it. In terms of minimum requirements you can discharge methane gas from a landfill into the atmosphere. Methane has a much higher greenhouse effect that carbon dioxide, so it would be better to burn it off from an environmental point of view. What this project will do is take it to a higher level than just the legislated minimum requirements. It is far better to use the gas than to burn it.

An environmental impact assessment showed that the landfill had minimal effect on air quality and health, but the industrial area next to the landfill does have an effect. So it will benefit the community if the emissions from industry can be reduced by replacing low grade fuel and recycled oil with a clean burning green energy source.

This project has been very useful. We can use the knowledge and the unbelievable contacts we have made. We have consultants approaching us about carbon credits but often we know more than they do now because our capacity has been built through this process. SouthSouthNorth are a team with very high ethical standards. We were initially concerned about their credentials as we did not know them, but trust builds up as you work together. We will continue to work together – we see this as the first of a number of projects.

JABAVU NKOMO AND PIERRE MUKHEBIR
The Helio Monitors, South Africa

The SouthSouthNorth projects are all energy efficiency related and have to do with the sustainable use of energy resources. Our brief is to monitor the development of the pilot projects for uniform methodology, accuracy of technical input, and adherence to Kyoto requirements. We observe and comment on all phases of the project cycle on issues involving both measuring and monitoring of data and process monitoring including, observance of the SouthSouthNorth sustainable development matrix, status of baselines, accuracy of technical data, robustness of financial data, public involvement, outreach and dissemination of outputs, quality of communication with the government authority, communication of SouthSouthNorth with project developers on pertinent issues, adequacy of staff in the team (skills, availability, etc.) and the creditworthiness of the owner. We sit with SouthSouthNorth in South Africa after every month to discuss progress. We attend project meetings held monthly and submit our reports to Helio International.

The Kuyasa Housing Project demonstrates clearly what the other projects should be doing. Project design teams meet regularly, ensuring active participation of community representatives. Local electricians, local plumbers and the community, with the assistance of a locally based energy company, were involved in the refitting the ten houses. This says something about the acquisition of skills and empowerment.

The value of the exercise has been to give an independent view of Clean Development Mechanism project development. Apart from simple monitoring, there have been workshops, meetings, conferences and the sharing of ideas. So the process has also been educational and very enlightening. The community has been involved in project development, with reasons given to them why things were being done the way they were. Involving the community has led to some employment, though temporary, and invaluable knowledge on energy efficiency. My main problem is that the concentration has been on the low income urban poor. They may understand the benefits of retrofits, and yet income may constrain them from doing what is desirable. Much value will be shown in later impact studies. At some point, after some months, one may want to track the economic, social and environmental value of the exercise with sufficient indicators for a detailed study.

Prof. Jabavu Clifford Nkomo, B.Sc. (Hons) Applied Economics (CNAA), M.Sc. (Economics) (Surrey), Ph.D. (Economics) (LSE, London), Energy and Development Research Centre, University of Cape Town. Prof. Nkomo has spent most of his working life teaching at universities where his areas of expertise are advanced economic theory, microeconomics, statistics, and mathematical economics. Although he majored in energy economics, his research interests include environmental economics, health economics and transport economics. He has done consultancy and research work in these areas for international agencies and government departments in Zimbabwe. Prof. Nkomo also served as Deputy Dean in the Faculty of Social Studies, University of Zimbabwe, as Dean, School of Business, University of Venda, and held Visiting Fellowships at Princeton University (USA) and the University of Oslo (Norway). He has been Director for the Road Motor Services under the National Railways of Zimbabwe, Essential National Health Information Research, Medical Research Council of Zimbabwe, the Zimbabwe Country Team on United Nations Framework Convention on Climatic Change, and National Research and Technology Foresight Project (Financial Services) for the Department of Arts and Culture in South Africa.

Pierre Mukhebir Pr.Eng., M.Sc. Civ. Eng. (Cape Town), H.Dip. Arb. (South African Association of Arbitrators), is a Registered Engineer and is currently a projects manager at Energy and Development Research Centre at the University of Cape Town responsible for the co-ordination of the energy research projects. He has been working in the field of rural development for the past ten years, doing both technical design and project management. He has experience in contract law and the resolution of contractual disputes. He is also accredited by Department of Public Works in Affirmative Procurement Procedures. He is currently researching the linkages between development and climate.

105

A SOUTHERN SYNERGY
work in progress

'I merged my notes together with dreams, imaginings. Naturally, they became
different from the original.'

Pramoedya Ananta Toer, *Indonesian novelist, 'This Earth of Mankind'*

106

These are SouthSouthNorth's stories from the developing world. They are fashioned from the truth of precision, notes, calculations mixed with the truth of ideals, dreams, imaginings. SouthSouthNorth is an emerging tapestry woven from the slender but resilient threads that link the countries of the South. These are fashioned by common histories, by particular relationships with the North, and by the desire to place Southern people and their economies at the centre of the global village. The centre of global gravity currently lies with the North, drawing the South towards a future not of its own choosing. The impending crisis of climate change is shifting this. The dry words of the Kyoto Protocol's Clean Development Mechanism have at their heart an originality that can write anew the rules of business and development.

This book records an odyssey of hope that I was privileged to be invited to join. I travelled three continents in rickshaws and bio-diesel trucks, on listing ferries, in aeroplanes that replace the safety instructions with a prayer sheet. I was carried across monsoon-flooded roads, invited to plant an Earth Day tree, walked on landfill sites evocative of Dante's inner circle of hell. I talked to scientists, lawyers, economists and hardworking, compassionate entrepreneurs. I read dense legal agreements and anthropological studies about when people switch their lights on and why. My mind stretched around patient explanations of the exhilarating potential for carbon trading to pay a premium for clean technology and sustainable development. I sat with children as they painted pictures of themselves and their environments. All of them expected their futures to be special. They are entitled to that belief.

An odyssey requires more, however, than the navigation skills needed for a physical journey. My compass was always the questions posed at the beginning of this book. What is sustainable development and how do you measure it? What is the best way to structure and manage projects? What draws in governments, investors, communities? How do you ensure benefits for the poorest in the South? With these I could trace SouthSouthNorth's quest into the uncharted waters of the Clean Development Mechanism. The answers are emerging from the specifics of finely tuned projects.

One of the strengths of SouthSouthNorth is its ability to contain and tap diversity and difference, finding the vibrancy, variety and ingenuity of the South to be an infinite source of capital. Drawing on this social and intellectual capital, SouthSouthNorth has learnt, and taught, many lessons about implementing the Clean Development Mechanism. Procedural lessons about ironing out bureaucratic wrinkles; lessons about fine-tuning technology; about calculating and monitoring carbon emissions and potential reductions; about reconciling fractious parties with different interests. I witnessed many lessons in practical altruism, from entrepreneurs and environmental activists alike. These challenge the cynical and unimaginative pragmatism of a global market that asks only for the lowest price and does not account for the real costs of how it does business.

This lyricism at the heart of rigorous science and profitable business made the journey wonderful.

The Clean Development Mechanism is
like a lemon, really like the seed of a
lemon. We had to make it grow, to water
it, to find the sugar, to make lemonade.
To make sure it is not too sour.

SouthSouthNorth:
that is what we do – we make lemonade.